Dedicated to the Rowan tree
and the goddess Brighid of the Flame

The First Aicme of
Voices from the Grove
(2020~2025)

The call of Elen,
The call of the wild.

The call of Brighid,
Bright inspiration.

The call of Bran,
And the Cauldron of Annwn.

The call of the Muse,
And the breath of nine maidens.

The call of Lugh,
Triumphant over darkness.

* * *

Beithe ~ Birch ~ Elen
New Beginnings and the Light of the land

Luis ~ Rowan ~ Brighid
Bright Inspiration and centred equilibrium

Fearn ~ Alder ~ Bran
Emotional Tranquility and the protection of the land

Saille ~ Willow ~ The Nine Maidens
Contemplation and the remembrance of all selves.

Nion ~ Ash ~ Lugh
Radiant Clarity over fear and darkness.

* * *

SHE WALKS IN SUNLIGHT

She walks by sunlight.
Spring at her feet,
Snow becoming grass,
Flowers bloom
At her approach.
She walks in serenity.
Birch trees lining the way
To the crib in the woods.
Sunlight kisses her hair
And it turns to gold.
She walks slowly,
Drinking in the mirth
Of the new born spring,
Rowan wreath shining
In her hair.
She walks by twilight,
Spear and shield,
Hammer and fire,
Life and death,
All in one.
Her eyes - blue as the sky,
Her face - lilies in bloom,
Her hair- sunlight and fire,
Proud and strong,
Glorious in her power.
Where she walks, winter ends,
Where she walks, life begins anew,
Where she walks, fire never dies,
Where she walks, children sleep
Peacefully at all times.
Brigid, daughter of Dagda,
Brigid, bright flame of Erin,
Brigid, flower of Imbolc,
Brigid, keeper of the hearth,
To you we sing.

by
Helena Sobolevskaya

3

Volume Two

of

VOICES FROM THE GROVE
(Beltane 2021 to Beltane 2022)

Ogham Diary and Journal

* * *

Celebrating the membership
of the Facebook Group

THE OGHAM GROVE

reaching 7000 members
(which happened in March – Full Moon in Elder - 2021)

Edited by Yuri Leitch

With deep gratitude to our Special Guests,
Gary Biltcliffe and Caroline Hoare, for their essays;
The Spirit of Brigid and the Fiery Arrow by Gary,
and *Awakening the Bride Consciousness in the Land* by Caroline.

With Contributions by Group Members
(in alphabetical order)

Corah Aplonia Avalon, Sheree Lynn Bailey, Thalia Brown,
Jenny Catalano, Kara Chambers, Naomi Cornock, Mary Ellen,
Roger Francis, Anthony Gammon, Claire Gerrard,
Lorraine Goodison, Kelly Grettler, Rosemary Hanson,
Gordon Harper, Tricia Hutchinson, Colleen Koziara,
Franklin LaVoie, Annie Louvaine, Jennifer Moore, Nell,
Alan Outten, Thea Prothero, Alison Pope, Bridee Redbud,
Nikki Shabbo, Tim Smyth, Helena Sobolevskaya,
Marc Rhodes-Taylor, Nia Walling, Gary Washington,
Ina Whistler, and Heidi Wyldewood.

Thank You

* * *

*
* * *

~ LIST OF CONTENTS ~

* * *

* * *

* * *
*

~ GREETINGS FROM THE EDITOR ~

Welcome to volume two of *Voices From The Grove*.

Each issue of 'The Grove' is dedicated to a deity that corresponds with a tree of the Ogham Grove. Volume one was dedicated to the goddess Elen of the Ways (for the Birch tree) and this volume is dedicated to Brighid and the fires of inspiration (for the Rowan tree).

Volume one contained quite a lot of Ogham lore, aimed at beginners (useful information worth having at hand), but rather than repeat it all over again I have abridged the text and created an Ogham Grove Archive; starting on page 194. The archive, and the Ogham Glossary on page 225, should give enough information to help any new readers make their way through the tangled briers of the Ogham Grove; and the contents of this journal.

In November 2020 The Ogham Grove group on Facebook reached a membership of 5000 members. To celebrate I came up with the idea of offering awards to my favourite submissions to this journal.

Three pieces of whittled work, from top to bottom,
a hand-painted Alder Wand,
an unpainted Hawthorn Stake,
and a small Ogham charm of Mistletoe wood.

Shown in the photo above: I offered a small Mistletoe charm with *Elen* painted upon it in Ogham; for my favourite poem. For my favourite piece of artwork – the unpainted Hawthorn Stake; and for my favourite essay/article, the Alder Wand. You will find the three winners throughout this journal.

I am not very comfortable creating a competition because how could I possibly be a fair panel of judges? It is just me choosing my favourites, which will always be subjective as beauty is in the eye of the beholder; but I'll give my reasons as to why I think something is worthy of special merit. That said, every entry in this journal is work that I respect and wish to promote, otherwise I would not have included it.

There has been a dynamic response with some wonderful examples of inspirational creativity; and I am very grateful. Some contributors are professionals in their field, and others are amateurs in the early stages of their creative journeys. If you like what you see then please take the next step and visit the contributors' own websites, or Facebook pages, to give them your encouragement.

My special guests for this volume of *The Grove* are the intrepid Earth Mysteries investigators, Gary Biltcliffe and Caroline Hoare – the authors of *The Spine of Albion*, and *The Power of* Centre; both highly recommended books if you are interested in the energies of the land and the spirits of place.

Caroline and Gary commissioned me to paint the artwork for the book covers of both of their books, and the cover of *The Power of Centre* (opposite) specifically pertains to the importance of the goddess Brighid and her lesser known role as Mother Goddess of the land; in Gary's own words,

'The front cover of our book, The Power of Centre, shows off the brilliant artwork of Yuri Leitch; depicting Brigid as the pregnant land goddess and Nut as a Celtic Sky goddess enveloping the British Isles and Ireland. Her triskele cross of straw connects three centres with the Isle of Man at the hub and all enclosed within the magical revolving ouroboros. Wherever there is a sacred landscape with defined ancient boundaries there is always something interesting at its middle or omphalos. In this book we explored the centre-points of many of the old Celtic lands and principalities around the British Isles and Ireland, and discovered remarkable places connected in some way with Bride, Brigid, Breeshay, or other derivatives of the Mother Goddess.'
(Gary's Facebook page)

I described Brighid as having the 'lesser known role as Mother Goddess of the land' because most readers will probably be more familiar with her as the saint of the Celtic Church, Bridget of Kildare – but she is much, much, more. The following essays will hopefully shed some much needed light upon our great goddess of whom the Christian saint is a beloved but much diminished echo - her true nature being the most 'High and Exalted One' of the Celts of the British Isles and Gaul. Known as Brigantia in Britain, and Brigindo in Gaul; a goddess of rivers, tribes, and towns; and the triumph of spring after the frozen harshness of winter. She is also intimately connected to the Ogham as she is both the sister of Ogma (the creator of the Ogham), and she is the goddess of divine poetic inspiration itself.

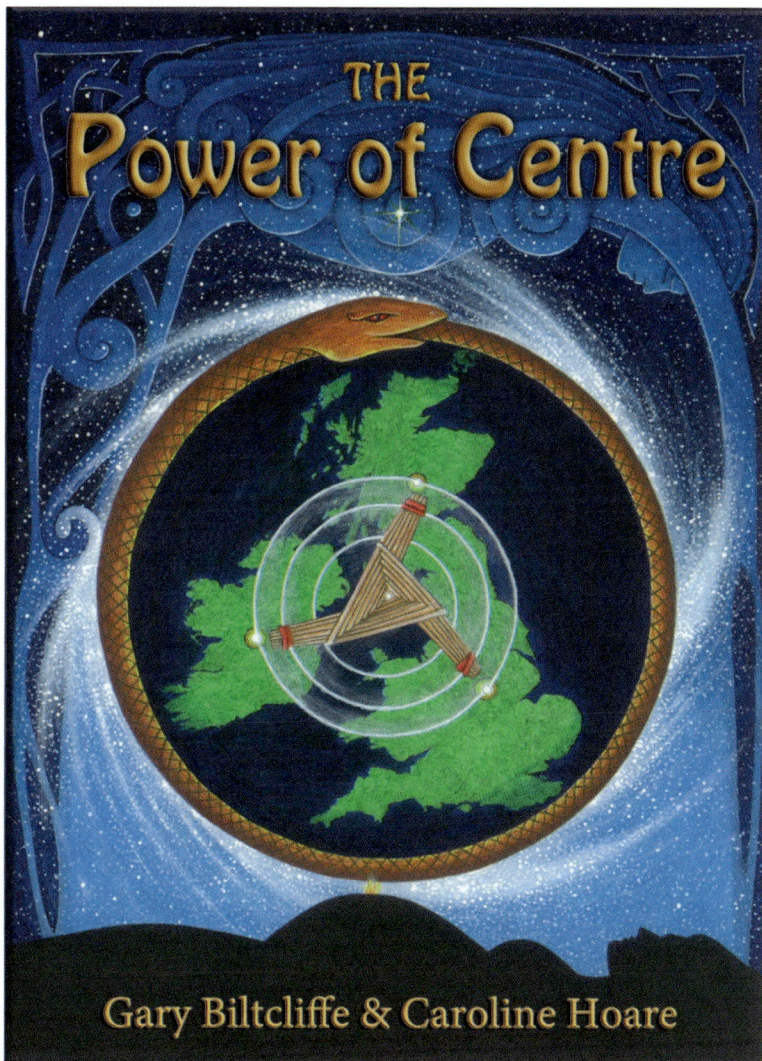

THE
Power of Centre

Gary Biltcliffe & Caroline Hoare

'*Esoteric practices require one to focus on the solar plexus or navel to find one's power centre. This is true within the landscape, and by finding its centre we find the focal place of power and therefore the most effective place to perform ceremony and healing. This we can also adapt to towns and cities. Taking from the old practices of worshipping the mother goddess Bride or Brigid and the elemental spirit of the land, we feel that by restoring, honouring and nourishing the centres of our nations, towns and cities, we can create harmony and balance once more, promoting good fortune, health and wellbeing to the land and its people.*'
(Gary Biltcliffe and Caroline Hoare, *The Power of Centre*)

~ THE CALL OF BRIGHID ~

'Brighid, Brid or Bridget of Ireland, Bride of Scotland, and Breeshay of the Isle of Man is an ancient Celtic goddess who has been venerated in different forms for over two and a half thousand years. Her presence was almost certainly felt in the ritual landscape that served the Avebury monument, as sarsen stones found scattered about the downs locally are referred to as Bridestones. Moreover, a potent local water source downhill from the West Kennet long barrow, known as Swallowhead Spring, which feeds the Kennet River, has been proposed as a site of her worship. In the past, heavy surface evaporation in the late summer would cause the spring to dry up, but in early February, around the Celtic feast of Bride, the sacred waters would miraculously gush forth once more signalling nature's return to life at the beginning of spring.'
(Andrew Collins, *The Cygnus Mystery*)

The above opening quote, from *The Cygnus Mystery* by Andrew Collins, comes from a chapter entitled *Goddess of the Swan*. Andrew's book is an astounding study that reveals just how very important Cygnus, the constellation of the swan, was to many ancient cultures; especially those of the British Isles. I'll say more about Cygnus further on.

The pagan gods and goddesses of Celtic Europe have been obscured by over fifteen-hundred years of Christianity. It is only in the last couple of centuries that they have really begun to re-emerge (thanks to archaeology and scholars of Celtic mythology). Many localised tribal deities have been lost completely but some greater deities, like Brighid, have left their mark so thoroughly upon the land and cultural psyche of the people that they can still stand sure in the 21st century; and beloved Brighid will stand proud for thousands of years yet to come as she is the natural Celtic figurehead for the coming Age of Aquarius – which will last for the next two-thousand years and more.

Knowledge of Brighid has survived in a number of different ways; not just as the triple goddess Brigid of Irish mythology (goddess of poetry, healing, and creativity), or her Christianised personification Saint Bridget, but also in the archaeological evidence for Brigantia, and the tribal people known as the Brigantes - and numerous locations that are named after her. On top of all of this there is the star-lore of the celestial swan and the great mother-goddess of the heavens. All of these facets of the divine feminine sing of her story and of her, eternal, presence.

Over the next few essays I shall explore some of the lore of our most 'high and exalted one' (for that is what her name means) and for the rest of this essay I'll present some star-lore that most probably pre-dates her archaeology and mythology; I'll also conclude with a look at her sacred tree, the beautiful Rowan.

In the Romano-British icon of Brigantia from Birrens (see the illustration on page 22) the goddess is depicted with an omphalos next to the bottom of her spear. An omphalos is a sacred stone that represents the navel (as in bellybutton) at the centre of any given territory; which can either be that of a sacred enclosure, or a country, or the entire world itself - and there is also the bellybutton of one's self, which was our direct connection to our own mothers when were were in the womb.

The omphalos thus declares Brigantia as governing a divine presence over the centre-point of a tribal territory (and a protective one at that, as she is equipped with both a spear and shield); but more significantly, the **central** area of the northern hemisphere night sky is full of Brighid related imagery.

The simplified star-map on the opposite page illustrates the primary constellations of The Milky Way in the northern hemisphere. As well as the main circumpolar stars (those that are ever-present), there are those at the top, the stars of the summer night sky, known as the Summer Triangle; and those at the bottom, are those of the winter night sky, the Winter Hexagram.

As will become apparent throughout the rest of this journal, all of the circumpolar constellations (and others) will be shown to correspond with Brighid-Brigantia. First of all the two bears (the Great Bear and the Little Bear – Ursa Major and Ursa Minor). The bear is considered a totem of Brighid because, as her festival of Imbolc marks the beginning of spring, so too do bears re-emerge after their winter hibernation when spring begins (and bears also love Rowan berries). The star called Polaris, of the Little Bear, marks the centre-point of the night sky; it is the pole-star of the current era – the omphalos of the starry realm.

The constellation of Draco the Dragon can be seen as a great serpent (and some ancient omphalos stones used to have serpents entwined around them – and the pole-star used to be one of Draco's stars). In Scottish Gaelic lore the 'Day of Bride' (Imbolc) was also equated with the emergence of a serpent from a hole (after its winter hibernation).

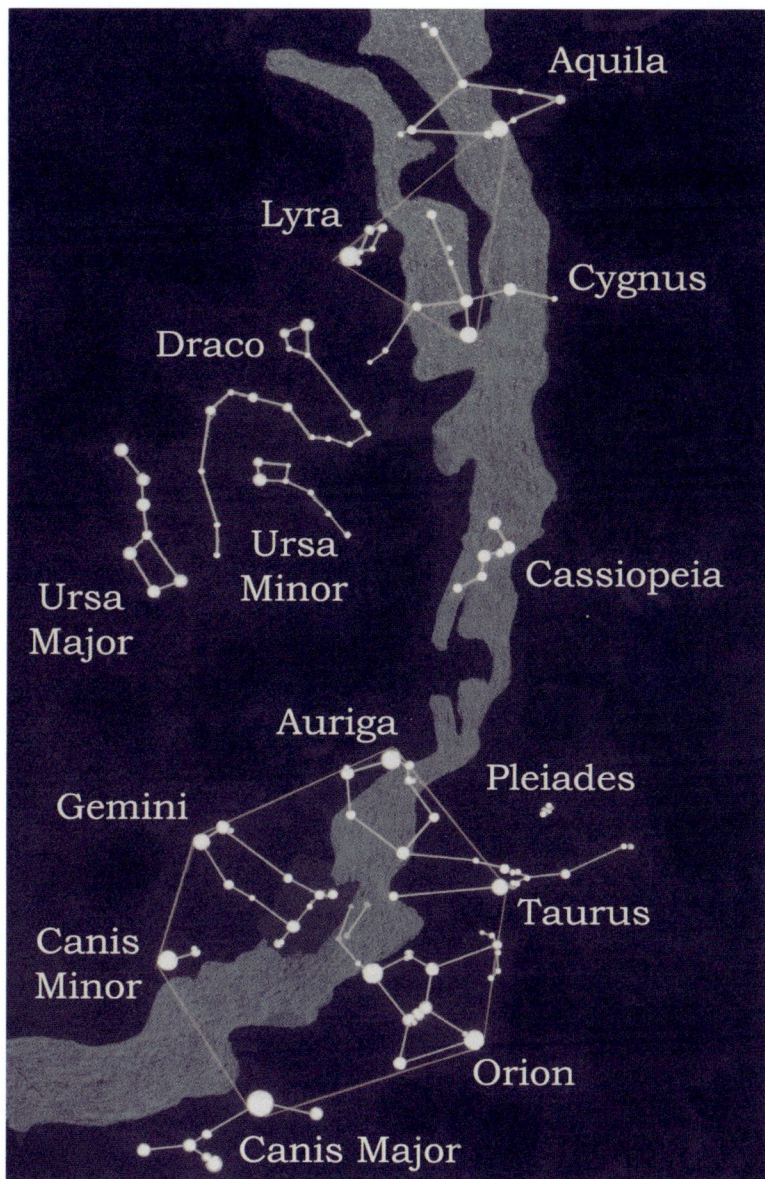

At the top of The Milky Way is the Summer Triangle, formed by Lyra, Cygnus, and Aquila.

In the central area are the Circumpolar Stars, Ursa Major, Draco, Ursa Minor, and Cassiopeia.

At the bottom, the Winter Hexagram of Canis Minor, Gemini, Auriga, Taurus, Orion, and Canis Major.

Probably the most important circumpolar constellation, (because it sits upon the **centre** of The Milky Way itself, betwixt the Winter Hexagon and the Summer Triangle), is that of Cassiopeia the Queen of Heaven. Its distinctive **W** shape has often been seen as representing a throne (when viewed sideways) and in Egypt it was the symbol of the goddess Isis (whose very name means 'throne'). But the **W** shape has also been seen as representing divine breasts; and the 'milky way' literally being the great river of milk from the mother-goddess. This breast symbolism is implied in the famous Gundestrup Cauldron.

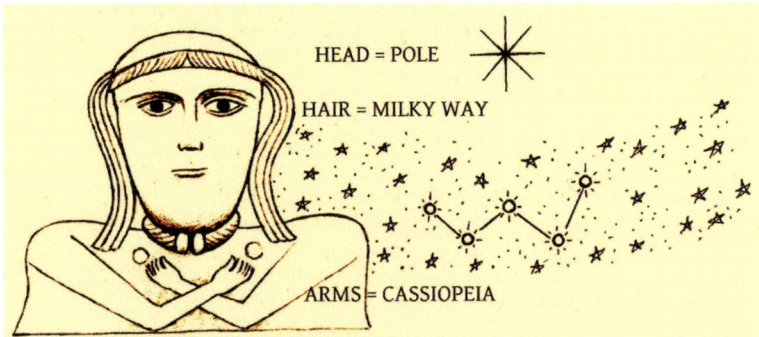

HEAD = POLE

HAIR = MILKY WAY

ARMS = CASSIOPEIA

Divine Female from the Gundestrup Cauldron, her arms making
the suggestive shape of the constellation of Cassiopeia.
Her chin has been badly damaged.

The constellation of Cassiopeia gives us a number of significant Brigantia-Brighid-Bride correspondences: firstly, evidence suggests that many rivers were named after Brigantia, and The Milky Way is the great river of the heavenly realm; secondly, Cassiopeia holds the centre-point between the winter and summer stars; thirdly, the constellation of the swan, Cygnus, is situated upon The Milky Way river as if accompanying Cassiopeia. In light of all of this it would seem reasonable to suggest that the constellation of Cassiopeia was a heavenly representation of Brigantia; her name means 'The High One' after all, and what could be higher than the centre of The Milky Way? Furthermore, upon a Romano-Celtic stone altar found at Corbridge (on Hadrian's Wall) there was an inscription dedicated to Brigantia; and upon it she was given the epithet of *Caelestis* which literally translates as 'heavenly, celestial'.

So much for the fixed stars, Brighid also holds a very unique celestial position in regards to the Arrow of Time; in the current and future centuries to come.

~ Cosmic Imbolc ~
and the
Goddess of the Aquarian Age

Whilst it may sound terribly 'New Agey', mother-ship planet Earth is in the process of transitioning from the Age of Pisces into the Age of Aquarius – which is a thing of factual observational astronomy – but what it means for humanity, spiritually and esoterically, is another thing entirely. The exact moment when the Age of Aquarius truly begins is a debatable question; but it will last for about 2500 years.

From a Celtic perspective, the primary deity of the Age of Aquarius will be Brigantia-Brighid-Bride because of her sacred festival of Imbolc occurring during the midpoint of the thirty degrees of Aquarius – Brighid is thus the destined goddess of the Aquarian Age (from a Celtic perspective); which also means that there will be a Cosmic Imbolc in about 1200 years time.

The Age of Aquarius is pretty big stuff; mind-blowing stuff really. What will the world be like, at the Cosmic Imbolc, twelve-hundred years from now? Will it be green and abundant? What will our descendants be like? Or indeed, how many reincarnations will we have before we experience that future moment in Time? (The Druids taught reincarnation). From now until that mysterious cosmic moment, and beyond, Brigantia-Brighid-Bride will be the Celtic goddess at the centre-point of the ever revolving heavens; and as without so within, so she is the mother-goddess of everyone's internal centre-point.

Brighid, she is at the centre of all of us.

~ ROWAN ~

The Rowan tree (also known as the Mountain Ash, and the Quicken Tree) has long been associated with St Bridget. It is the second tree of the Ogham and in the astrological year wheel of the Ogham Grove it spans the sun's journey from the 27th degree of Capricorn through to the 15th degree of Aquarius - the exact cross-quarter day (mid-point) between the Winter Solstice and the Spring Equinox; better known as Imbolc (the feast day of St Bridget, St Bride).

Both Imbolc and Rowan are sacred to the goddess Brighid; and she is the sister of Ogma (the creator of the Ogham) – one of her main attributes is that of goddess of poets and poetic inspiration. The symbol of modern Druidry, the Awen, represents rays of poetic inspiration; and these rays are also referred to as Brigit's flaming arrows of inspiration, or simply, her 'fiery arrows'.

Rowan is a beautiful tree, and it is the first tree of the Rose-family pentagram (which is governed by Apple holding the position of Summer Solstice). Rowan berries have little black five-pointed stars upon them; making Rowan a goddess-blessed tree of protection. Rowan trees were often planted in the corner of farmer's fields to protect their land and animals – and this may be one explanation for the Medieval Briatharogam kenning, 'friend of cattle'. Rowan was used by farmers to protect their livestock from harm by witchcraft; and the berries can be dried and worn as beads – as protective charms.

16

ROWAN

Imbolc

Bright red berries

Berries have black five-pointed stars

Rowan leaves are on the stem

Ash leaves have stems of their own

long

Leaves are toothed

Leaves are 'pinnate,' formed in opposite pairs

ROWAN ASH

ROWAN IS ALSO KNOWN AS 'MOUNTAIN ASH' BUT HAS BRIGHT RED BERRIES + THE ASH HAS NO BERRIES AT ALL

Simple motif

The call of Brighid, bright inspiration.
Protection of the Rowan,
From its star-blessed berries.
Peace at the sacred centre;
The centre of all beings.

~ BRIGANTIA, GODDESS OF THE CELTS ~

This essay is about the archaeological and historical evidence for the goddess Brigantia; of whom Brigid of the Tuatha Dé Danann, and Saint Bridget of the early Celtic Church, are but much later divine and sacred expressions. Theoretically, the mythology of Brigid should pre-date that of Saint Bridget but it was not recorded until long after the ascent of Christianity (and it was recorded by Christian scribes – the time-line on the opposite page presents the basic evidence in its chronological order).

The Iron Age Celtic tribes did not leave any written evidence about their gods and goddesses. As frustrating as it may be, we are thus forced to observe Celtic spirituality through the eyes of the Roman Empire; but over the many centuries of Roman rule the Romanised Celts of Britain and Gaul did succeed in leaving us a vast wealth of statues, iconography, and Latin inscriptions – which means that well known names of gods and goddesses (like Cernunnos and Brigantia) are actually Latinised names rather than their original Celtic ones (for instance, the origin of Brigantia may simply have been something like *BRIG* and it was probably pronounced 'breeg' – although each tribe would have had its own regional dialect).

There are at least eight known inscriptions to Brigantia in the British Isles; and one also describes her as 'heavenly, celestial', and another calls her a 'divine nymph' (a river goddess). A number of rivers are thought to have been named after Brigantia, including the Braint in Anglesey and the Brent in Middlesex. Fresh flowing water is sacred; quite simply it the fuel of life, and there are a great many holy wells dedicated to St Bridget, and St Bride, that probably originated as sacred water sanctuaries of Brig-Brigantia.

'... goddesses who are especially concerned with rivers. We may assume their temples to have been at the sources of these, and although no evidence for such is as yet forthcoming, the constant references in the early Irish tales to buildings being erected over sacred wells, the sources of rivers, may suggest that some sort of shrines in such situations were known in Britain and Gaul.'
(Anne Ross, *Pagan Celtic Britain*)

BRIGANTIA-BRIGHID-BRIDE TIME-LINE

Since the most ancient of days ~ the star-lore of the constellation known as Cassiopeia represented the life-giving breasts of the mother-goddess, situated upon The Milky Way, **centred** between the stars of summer and the stars of winter (and she is eternally accompanied by Cygnus the Swan).

200 BC to 300 AD ~ The late Iron Age Gundestrup Cauldron depicts a Divine Female holding a Cassiopeia posture (and the cauldron is also decorated with many other examples of star-lore).

1st century AD ~ Celtic tribes recorded by early Roman writers:
the Brigantii tribe of the Alps,
the Brigantes of northern Britain,
and the Brigantes of southern Ireland.

1st century AD ~ the 'Brigitte' statue of Brigindo (Brigantia), now at the Museum of Brittany, depicts the goddess wearing a swan-adorned helmet.

1st century AD ~ the history of the British queen of the Brigantes, Cartimandua, suggests that the Brigantes were a matriarchal society; and named after their mother-goddess, Brig-Brigantia.

2nd century AD ~ the fine-detailed stone icon of Brigantia from the Roman fort of Blatobulgium, of modern day Birrens in Dumfriesshire, southern Scotland.

Brigid, goddess of the Tuatha Dé Danann, is of pre-Christian Celtic mythology but her written evidence arrives late.

Saint Bridget of Kildare is usually said to have lived between 451 AD and 525 AD; her feast day is the 1st of February.

7th century AD ~ the *Vita Sanctae Brigitae* (Life of St Brigid) was written by Cogitosus (a monk of Kildare) around 650 AD; and this is the earliest evidence for the existence of Saint Bridget.

10th century AD ~ *Sanas Cormaic* ('Cormac's Glossary') describes Brigid as a triple goddess of protection, poetry, and healing.

11th century AD ~ the *Lebor Gabála Érenn* (The Book of the Taking of Ireland) describes Brigid as a daughter of the Dagda, and goddess of poetry (inspirational wisdom).

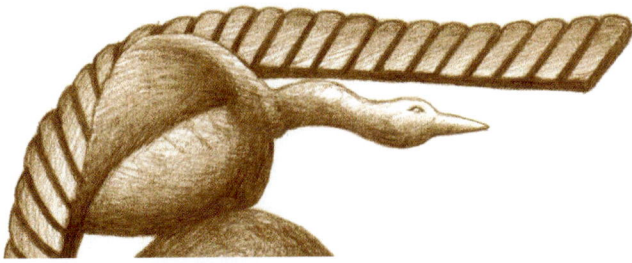

Above ~ map of the Celtic tribes of the 1st century AD; painted by Alan Royce of Glastonbury. See the Brigantes of northern Britain and also of south-east Ireland – they may have been the same people upon either side of the Irish Sea coastal sea trade.

Opposite ~ the statue of 'Brigitte' from the Museum of Brittany is thought to date to the 1st century AD. Her helmet is adorned with a swan carrying a long serpentine plume – could this represent the constellation of Cygnus the Swan upon the great river of The Milky Way?

BRIGANTIA
From Birrens, Dumfriesshire, southern Scotland.

The image opposite is the best known icon of Brigantia in the British Isles. She dates to the early 2nd century AD; and she is heavily decorated as the Roman goddess Minerva – although its inscription clearly declares her to be Brigantia. The Romans tended to equate all powerful goddesses with Minerva. This stone icon comes from Dumfriesshire, which was the northern territory of the Celtic tribe known as the Brigantes.

'We may also consider Cartimandua herself, powerful queen of a powerful tribe, united under her leadership and invoking, not a god, but the great goddess Brigantia, 'High One'. In this type of Celtic ruler-queen then, mother, mate and politician, strategist and combatant in war, we may visualise some earthly reflection of the cult concept of the 'Mother of the Gods'.'
(Anne Ross, *Pagan Celtic Britain*)

The Roman system of religious interpretation, known as *Interpretatio Romana*, equated Brigantia with Minerva (who actually corresponds very well with the Irish goddess Brigid because they are both goddesses of poetry, healing, and smith-crafts). Minerva's symbol is the Owl of knowledge, and she is usually depicted with a spear, shield, and helmet (she was celebrated by Rome as the goddess of intellect and successful military strategy – defense and protection rather than conquest). Archaeology has revealed at least nineteen dedications to Minerva throughout Britain, and whilst it is unlikely that they all represented Brigantia, they are certainly evidence of the Celts having a strong belief in powerful goddesses. Minerva had a significant presence at the town of Aquae-Sulis (Bath) where three dedications to her have been found - at the sacred healing waters of the Celtic goddess Sulis (who is also known as Sul). Brigantia and Sulis were both goddesses of sacred waters and they were both worshipped in the guise of Minerva.

'The fact that Brigantia is called nymph-goddess on an inscription from near Irthington is not in any way out of keeping with this Celtic tradition of associating the territorial goddess especially with sacred wells and streams.'
(Anne Ross, *Celtic Pagan Britain*)

There is no substantial written lore about Brigantia; other than the inscriptions that refer to her as 'celestial' and 'divine nymph' (and that her name means 'Most High' or the 'High One' - which of course is a vague honorary descriptive rather than a proper name). Some scholars see 'Brigit' (the honorary title) as an epithet for the mother of the gods – known as Dana in Ireland and Dón in Britain; but in the earliest Irish manuscripts she is described as being the daughter of the Dagda (the good god); and as a sibling to other deities like Ogma the creator of the Ogham.

'The Dagda had several children, the most important of whom are Brigit, Angus, Mider, Ogma, and Bodb the Red. Of these, Brigit will be already familiar to English readers who know nothing of Celtic myth. Originally she was a goddess of fire and the hearth, as well as of poetry, which the Gaels deemed an immaterial, supersensual form of flame. But the early Christianizers of Ireland adopted the pagan goddess into their roll of saint-ship, and, thus canonized, she obtained immense popularity as Saint Bridget, or Bride.'
(Charles Squire, *Celtic Myth & Legend: Poetry & Romance*)

There are numerous place names throughout Britain that are named after Bridget or Bride, and this is very curious because Saint Bridget of Kildare was not an evangelising saint (that is, she is not known to have travelled so widely as to leave her mark on so many places – thus those places are most likely named after the 'High One' (Brig) rather than the saint of Ireland).

BRIGHID

'Brigit, the goddess of fire, poetry, and the hearth, is famous today as Saint Bridget, or Bride. Most popular of all the Irish saints, she can still be easily recognized as the daughter of the Dagda. Her Christian attributes, almost all connected with fire, attest her pagan origin. She was born at sunrise; a house in which she dwelt blazed into a flame which reached to heaven; a pillar of fire rose from her head when she took the veil; and her breath gave life to the dead. As with the British goddess Sul, worshipped at Bath, who – the first century Latin writer Solinus tells us - "ruled over the boiling springs, and at her altar there flamed a perpetual fire which never whitened into ashes, but hardened into a stony mass," the sacred flame on her shrine at Kildare was never allowed to go out.'
(Charles Squire, *Celtic Myth & Legend: Poetry & Romance*)

The earliest written evidence about the goddess Brigid of the Tuatha Dé Danann comes from a 10ᵗʰ century Irish dictionary known in English as *Cormac's Glossary*. The following quote is taken from the 1868 translation by Irish scholars John O'Donovan and Whitley Stokes,

'BRIGIT: i.e. a poetess, daughter of the Dagda. This is Brigit the female sage, or woman of wisdom, i.e. Brigit the goddess whom poets adored, because very great and very famous was her protecting care. It is therefore they call her goddess of poets by this name. Whose sisters were Brigit the female physician (woman of leechcraft), Brigit the female smith (woman of smithwork); from whose names with all Irishmen a goddess was called Brigit. Brigit, then, 'breo-aigit, breo-shaigit' 'a fiery arrow'.'

Brigit's divine qualities, shared with the Roman goddess Minerva, are immediately perceptible – she is '*the female sage, or woman of wisdom*' and she was famous for her '*protecting care*' (spear and shield). But more than this, and typically Celtic, Brigit is described as having two sisters who were also called Brigit,

Brigit of Poetry
Brigit of Healing
Brigit of Smithwork

It is this insight that makes Brigit a triple goddess; and as *Cormac's Glossary* states, '*with all Irishmen a goddess was called Brigit*'. Again, 'Brig' is just an honorary title that means 'most high'. So Brighid of the Tuatha Dé Danann was a three-fold goddess of wisdom and protection; as well as of poetic inspiration, healing, and creativity – and as she was far too important (and beloved) to be forsaken, she was absorbed into the Celtic Church as Saint Bridget of Kildare.

IMBOLC

The feast day of Saint Bridget is the 1ˢᵗ February, which is also the pagan fire festival of Imbolc – the 'first day of spring' and mid-point between the Winter Solstice and the Spring Equinox. In Old Irish *i-mbolc* means 'in the belly' and it is thought to pertain to new lambs about to be born (but it is also worth contemplating the omphalos, navel, centre-point, significance to the great goddess 'Most High'.

LUIS
(Rowan)

by Yuri Leitch

An illustration for book one of
The Chronicles of Ogus

The modern day interest in Celtic mysticism really kicked off during the 1800s, and the late Victorian enthusiasm for Celtic art and literature is often referred to as the Celtic Twilight – which is a title taken from a book by the Irish poet William Butler Yeats; *The Celtic Twilight*, which was published in 1893.

As well as being a key mover in the Irish Literary Revival (a group of visionaries and mystics that sought to breath new life into old gods and call forth the return of the Fae) W. B. Yeats was also a significant member of the Western Magical Tradition that was dynamic in London during the cusp of the 19th and 20th centuries.

The end of one century and the beginning of another is a fascinating window in time, and it makes many mystically inclined people ponder the meaning of the end of the old and the beginning of the new. There were many ideas about a coming new age; one was called The Age of Michael (the archangel, which had apparently begun in 1879) and another, more tangible age, was that of the Age of Aquarius – but when it was to begin was uncertain; as it depended upon which method you used to measure it.

One now quite famous occult society was created with the dawn of the new age in mind – the Hermetic Order of the Golden Dawn - was established in 1887; and W. B. Yeats became one of its most significant members. Another Celtic revivalist, and a good friend of Yeats, was William Sharp; and he too was a member of the Golden Dawn. Sharp was a very gifted psychic, and he and Yeats spent many years exploring psychical research together. William Sharp was dedicated to the Gaelic mysticism of Scotland and Ireland, and under the literary pseudonym of Fiona Macleod he produced many hauntingly beautiful books.

'The Celtic mission of Yeats and Sharp was very different to the pro-Christian Sun-worshipping Bardo-Druidism of William Stukeley and Iolo Morganwg; Yeats and Sharp did not seek to reinvent Celtic spirituality. They delved deep into the lore of the pagan

Celtic gods and goddesses and attempted to resurrect the all but forgotten deities of the British Isles. W. B. Yeats hints at their great effort in the following poem.

The Valley of the Black Pig

The dew drops slowly and dreams gather: unknown spears
Suddenly hurtle before my dream-awakened eyes,
And then the clash of fallen horsemen and the cries
Of unknown perishing armies beat about my ears.
We who still labour by the cromlech on the shore,
The grey cairn on the hill, when day sinks drowned in dew,
Being weary of the world's empires, bow down to you,
Master of the still stars and of the flaming door.'

(Yuri Leitch, *Gwyn, God of Annwn: Druidic Star-Lore and the Bardic Mysteries*)

Fiona Macleod was a lot more than simple pen-name for William Sharp, rather, she was a very real personality in her own right. The issue is a complicated one, and having read Elizabeth Sharp's intimate memoirs of her husband's life, one is left uncertain as to the true metaphysical nature of 'Fiona' – was she William's alter-ego, a type of split-personality? Or was she one of his own past-lives? Or was she an otherworldly spirit-entity attracted by the psychical work that William had participated in with W. B. Yeats? In many ways it does not matter, the material written under the personality of Fiona Macleod is rich in fascinating Celtic lore; but one cannot consider it to be anything other than 19th century speculation. Here is a sample of the Fiona Macleod material,

'St. Brighid (in Gaelic pronounced sometimes 'Bride', sometimes 'Breed'), St. Bride of the isles as she is lovingly called in the Hebrides, has no name so dear to the Gael as 'Muime-Chriosd', Christ's Foster-Mother, a name bestowed on her by one of the most beautiful of Celtic legends. In the Isles of Gaelic Scotland her most familiar name is 'Brighid nam Bratta' – St. Briget or St. Bride of the Mantle – from having wrapt the new-born Babe in her Mantle in Mary's hour of weakness. She did not come into the Gaelic heart with the Cross and Mary, but was there long before as Bride,

Brighid, or Brithid of the Dedannans, those not immortal but for long ages deathless folk who to the Gael were as the Olympians to the Greeks. The earlier Brighid was goddess of poetry and music, one of the three great divinities of love, goddess of women, the keeper of prophecies and dreams, the watcher of the greater destinies, the guardian of the future. I think she was no other than a Celtic Demeter – the Demeter-Desphoena born of the embrace of Poseidon, who in turn is no other than Lir, the Oceanus of the Gael: and instead of Demeter seeking and lamenting Persephone in the underworld, it is Demeter-Brighid seeking her brother (or, it may be, her son) Manan (Manannan), God of the Sea, son of Oceanus, Lir – and finding him at last in Iceland, etc. - as I write here a little further on. Persephone and Manan are symbols of the same Return of Life.

The other names are old Gaelic names: 'Brighid Muirghin-no-tuinne', Brighid-Conception-of-the-Waves; 'Brighid-Sluagh' (or 'Sloigh'), Brighid of the Immortal Host; 'Brighid-nan-Sitheachseang', Brighid of the Slim Fairy Folk; 'Brighid-Binne-Bheul-lhuchdnan-trusganan-uaine', Song-sweet (lit. melodious mouth'd) Brighid of the the Tribe of the Green Mantles. She is also called Brighid of the Harp, Brighid of the Sorrowful, Brighid of Prophecy, Brighid of Pure Love, St. Bride of the Isles, Bride of Joy, and other names.'

(Fiona Macleod; *The Winged Destiny, Studies in the Spiritual History of the Gael*)

For Fiona Macleod, Brighid was the great goddess of the Gaelic pagan world, and equal to Great Isis of Egypt herself; which is intriguing when considering that the constellation of Cassiopeia was also known as the Throne of Isis. Do the Fiona Macleod writings tap into ancient esoteric lore? The reader must decide for themselves. Her writings are certainly potent and inspirational.

'... before ever the first bell of Christ was heard by startled Druids coming across the hills and forest lands of Gaul, the Gaels worshipped a Brighde or Bride, goddess of women, of fire, of poetry. When, today, a Gaelic islesman alludes to Briget of the Songs, or when a woman of South Uist prays to Good St. Bride to bless the empty cradle that is soon to be filled, or when a 'shennachie' or teller of tales speaks of an oath taken by Briget of the Flame, they refer, though probably unconsciously, to a far older Brighid than they who speak with loving familiarity of 'Muime Chriosd', Christ's Foster Mother, or 'Brighid-nam-Bratta', St. Bride

of the Mantle. **They refer to one who in the dim, far-off days of the forgotten pagan world of our ancestors was a noble great goddess. They refer to one to whom the women of the Gael went with offerings and prayers, as went the women of ancient Hellas to the temples of Aphrodite, as went the Syrian women to the altars of Astarte, as went the women of Egypt to the milk-fed shrines of Isis.'**
(Fiona Macleod, *St Briget of the Shores*)

Just before the turn of the century, in 1898, a rather eccentric mystical Christian, Dr John Arthur Goodchild, published his inspired (but highly questionable) history of the British Isles, *The Light of the West*. Simplistically, Dr Goodchild believed that Christianity had lost its way because it was purely patriarchal, and he believed that a revitalised Celtic Church should bring about the return of the divine feminine – he believed that the Great Goddess of the Celtic West was destined to be the 'Bride' (pun intended) of Christ in a new golden era. In *The Light of the West* Goodchild gave quite a few quotes from the writings of Fiona Macleod; here is one example.

'St Bridget, the best known of Ireland's female saints, was soon draped by the monks in all that they could borrow from that Brigh (the Bride), after whom she was named. Brigh was the Bright One, the Angel of Purity and Peace, the patroness of song and psalmody. In the legends of the Western Isles much of the teachings of Brigh still remain, as evident in Fiona Macleod's beautiful story, 'Muime Chriosd' the foster-mother of Christ. It is probable that such legends have led men like the late Mr. Perceval, son of the Prime Minister, into the idea that the Virgin Mary herself was buried in Ireland, but they are founded upon the Messianic prophecies of the Bride.'
(J. A. Goodchild, *The Light of the West*)

Dr Goodchild was a friend of William Sharp, although it is unlikely that he realised that Sharp and Fiona Macleod were one and the same person; as William Sharp kept his secret very well – it appears that only his wife and sister were in on it. They were also quite different men; Sharp (Fiona) sang about Bride as a pre-Christian pagan goddess, and Goodchild deliberately turned a blind-eye away from any inherent paganism. One can imagine William's private amusement when listening to Goodchild sing the praises of Fiona Macleod – that said, their friendship seems to have been a genuine one.

Dr Goodchild's own esoteric ponderings were strongly influenced by his contemplations of the world transitioning from the Age of Pisces into the Age of Aquarius; and he knew that in the classical mythologies (those of Greece and Rome) Aquarius was sacred to the Queen of the Gods:

CLASSICAL PERSONIFICATIONS OF AQUARIUS

Roman ~ Juno, the Queen of the Gods
Greek ~ Hera, the Queen of the Gods

And so he looked for a Celtic equivalent of Juno and Hera; and he believed he found her in the Irish goddess, the Morrighan, whose name he translated as 'Mor-Rigan' (Great Queen) which he considered to be a title for Brighid-Bride (which not many scholars would agree with).

In combination with this he also realised that the time of year when the Sun is in the sign of Aquarius corresponds with the Celtic festival of Imbolc; which, rather perfectly, is specifically sacred to Brighid.

In 1904, at the beginning of August, William Sharp and Dr Goodchild met up with each other in Glastonbury, England. They visited an area to the west of the town, known as St Brides, and a man-made water feature (actually a field sluice) that Dr Goodchild insisted on calling 'St Bride's Well' (for his own esoteric purposes). They also visited a nearby earthwork, the 'Beckery Salmon' that Goodchild considered to be a representation of the famous Salmon of Wisdom; of Celtic tradition. All very strange indeed and it is a very long story.

Simplistically, Goodchild was playing with the land around Glastonbury, in an inspired way, motivated by the transition of the Age of Pisces into the Age of Aquarius. The 'Beckery Salmon' represented Pisces the Fish, and 'St Bride's Well' corresponded with Aquarius the Water-bearer. (There are of course numerous Bride's Wells throughout the British Isles, and Brigantia was seen as a divine nymph and goddess of rivers – and as has already been explained, Bride is the natural Celtic divinity for the Age of Aquarius).

The eastern horizon, as viewed from Goodchild's 'St Bride's Well', is dominated by Glastonbury Tor – which, being opposite Bride's Aquarian well, makes the Tor correspond with Leo the Lion. By default then, Glastonbury Abbey being opposite the Pisces Salmon, corresponds with Virgo (and it is dedicated to the **Virgin** Mary). Quite brilliantly (and here is Goodchild's genius vision) between Glastonbury Tor and Glastonbury Abbey is a hill called Chalice Hill (and between the signs of Leo and Virgo is a secondary constellation called Crater the Cup (the Chalice).

Goodchild's landscape mysticism used the cusp of the Age of Pisces and the Age of Aquarius to tap into Glastonbury's already well established Holy Grail, and Saint Bridget, traditions. (The whole Goodchild intrigue is rich in other complexities and if you are interested in learning more, please see my book *The Terrestrial Alignments of Katharine Maltwood and Dion Fortune*. My purpose for mentioning it here is to demonstrate the influence of Brighid upon the intrigues of modern world Celtic mysticism).

The diagram at the top of the next page demonstrates how the constellation of Crater the Cup is positioned directly opposite the cusp between Pisces and Aquarius; and the ever-flowing waters of the sign of the Queen of the Gods perpetually flow downward into the 'Heavenly Grail'.

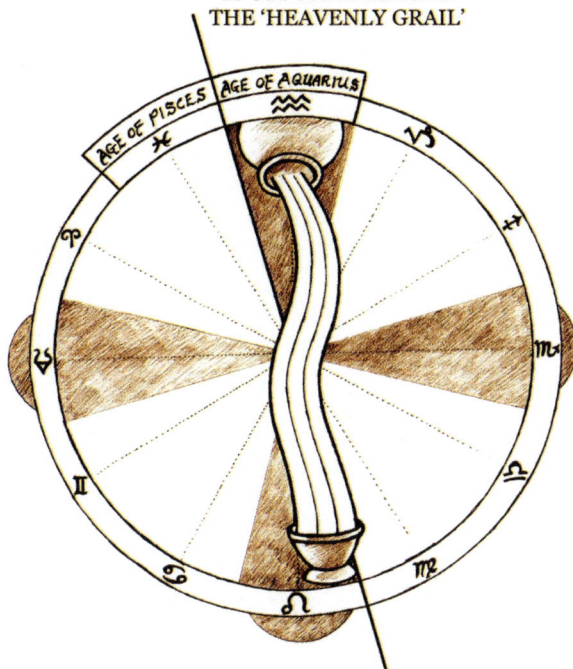

THE TRANSITIONAL CUSP
BETWEEN PISCES AND AQUARIUS
IS OPPOSITE CRATER
THE 'HEAVENLY GRAIL'

In 1912, a friend of Dr Goodchild, Miss Alice Buckton, purchased a large property with land at the foot of Chalice Hill, Glastonbury, and she gave it the name of Chalice Well; and which is now a very popular sanctuary to many of the town's visitors. Goodchild died in 1914 but Alice Buckton had become very inspired by, and involved with, his esoteric landscape intrigues. Within fourteen years of William Sharp and Goodchild observing the Tor as Leo, and the abbey of Glastonbury as Virgo, (with Chalice Hill between them corresponding with the constellation of Crater the Cup - as viewed from 'St Bride's Well') – Miss Buckton established for all time, Chalice Well (which is a real well and not a field sluice) at the foot of Chalice Hill beside Glastonbury Tor. Furthermore, Alice Buckton promoted Chalice Well as being an Aquarian well; and she was, as Goodchild had been, a devoted enthusiast for St Bride.

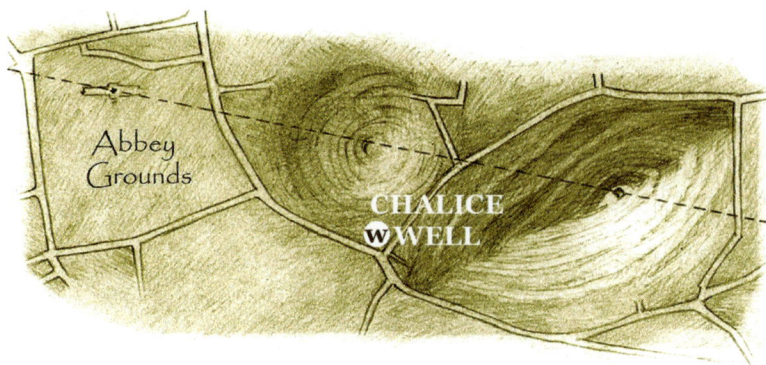

In 1918 Alice Buckton published a book of her own poetry, called *Daybreak and Other Poems;* and the frontpiece of which was the following poem – the 'Water-Bearer' is the sign of Aquarius, of course, and the 'bride and bridegroom' are Goodchild's new Celtic matriarchal faith and the established patriarchal church.

AT THE WELL
The Rune of the Water-Bearer

Ye have supped from the Pools of Sorrow,
Ye shall drink from the Wells of Joy!
The Golden Wheel is turning -
The heavenly spheres' employ!

And she that bears the Measure
Shall stand in the Dawn of Day,
Pouring the waters of comfort
To the weary by the way.

Haste, O bride and bridegroom!
Behold the promised Sign!
The hand that draws the Water
Has filled the Cup with Wine.
(Alice Buckton, *Daybreak*, 1918)

At the back of *Daybreak* Alice Buckton also included a play that she had written, called *The Coming of Bride*, which is a fictional piece about the life of the saint and her visit to Glastonbury in the 5th century; it is quaint and Christian, and it ends with Bride predicting the coming of King Arthur and his knights of the Round Table (to connect Bride with the mystery of the Holy Grail).

In 1935, Katharine Maltwood published her book about her discovery of the Glastonbury Zodiac – within the scheme of which Glastonbury Tor is part of a vast phoenix effigy with Chalice Well representing the Aquarian waters flowing from its beak – an evolution of Dr Goodchild's zodiacal landscape intrigues?

'The Water Bearer effigy, of Glastonbury's Isle of Avalon, resembles a Phoenix with outstretched wings, turning its head to reach the lifegiving waters of the Chalice Well Blood Spring; for the Druid's well forms the Urn of this Aquarius, and has always been associated with the Holy Grail.'
(Katharine Maltwood, *Temple of the Stars*)

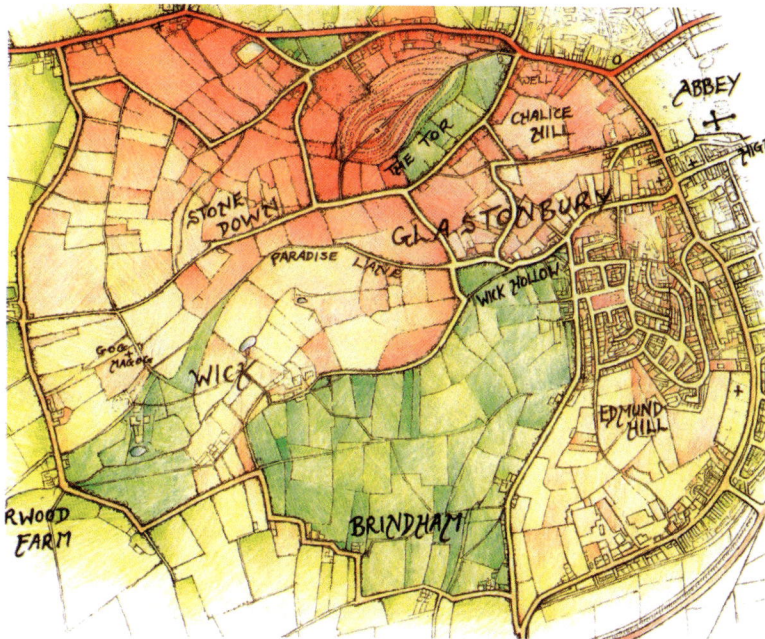

The Lady Dindraine
By Yuri Leitch
from the Well Maidens of the Summerlands project

wellmaidens.co.uk

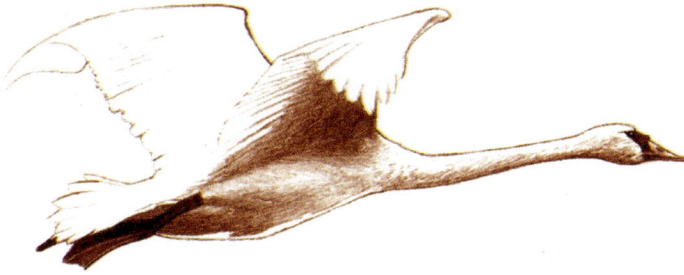

Brighid-Bride now has a definite presence in modern day Glastonbury; although most visitors are unaware of the esoteric intrigues of the past. Bride's Mound, the land near Dr Goodchild's 'St Bride's Well' (field sluice) is now a protected area, nature reserve, that is looked after by The Friends of Bride's Mound,

www.friendsofbridesmound.com

It is a beautiful area, a vantage point from where deer can be seen running across the Somerset Levels; and of course it has a great view of Glastonbury Tor in the east. The Friends of Bride's Mound have planted an avenue of Wild Cherry and Rowan trees there; it is a sacred place.

There is a Bridget Healing Centre in the centre of town; that specialises in shamanic studies,

www.bridgethealingcentre.co.uk

And of course there is Chalice Well itself; and I am sure it will always be there - the Aquarian Age waters of Brighid beside Glastonbury Tor.

www.chalicewell.org.uk

* * *

To A Rowan Tree
Leaning over a Low-Walled Garden
* * *

Fair slender Ash uplifted
Against the blue,
Your blood-bright berries glistening
With morning dew!

You carry my thoughts afar
To a lonely glen,
Where antlered ferns go down
To a rushy fen,

And mix in the western waves
Of a watered shore,
Within the sound of the deep
Atlantic roar...

There, amid mossy stone,
And hoary stem,
I marvel to see a Thing
Apart from them -

Over a dark pool bending
As from the skies,
A vision of beauty dreaming
In Paradise,

Dropping berries slow
In the waters clear!
And listening under the leaves
Again I hear

The holy Druid tale
Of the country-side,
Of Connla's hidden Well
And sweet Saint Bride!
* * *

by Alice M. Buckton

from her book
Daybreak and Other Poems
published in 1918
(founder of the Chalice Well gardens, Glastonbury)

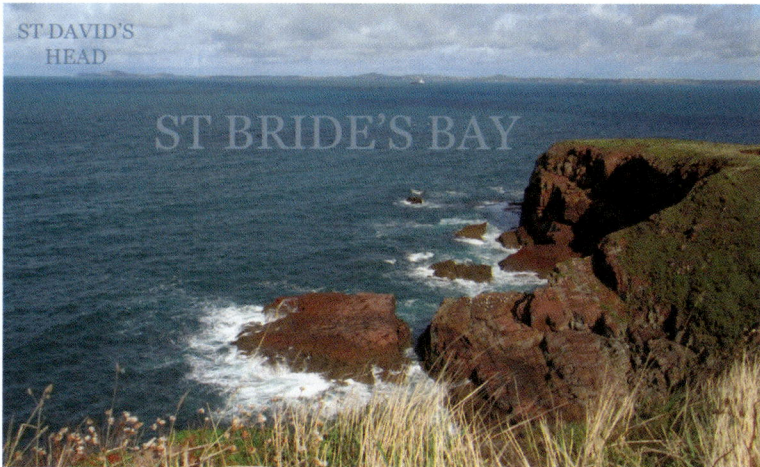

In September 2017, a good friend and I travelled all the way from Glastonbury to St Bride's Bay in Pembrokeshire (south-west Wales) by car. It took us a lot longer than it looked like it would on our road-map – maybe at least six hours of driving (fortunately we had booked to stay the night at a Youth Hostel). Neither of us had been to St Bride's Bay before. It has a beautiful and mostly unspoilt coast-line, and it is a part of the Pembrokeshire Coast National Park; and it is protected under European environmental law as a special area of conservation.

My friend's birthday is the 1st February, the feast day of Saint Bride, and we specifically intended to visit the small coastal village of St Bride's; to see what we could see and to make a heart-mind connection with the place.

St Brides, the place, is very small; it is a parish and a tiny coastal village. There is very little there, it is just a small bay with a church, a couple of fisherman's cottages, and a 19th century manor house that is now known as St Bride's Castle; and which has been converted for use as luxury holiday accommodation.

St Bride's Bay is the furthest west of Wales. It is located in the territory that belonged to a Celtic tribe known as the Demetae. The tribal seat of the Demctae, in Roman times, was Moridunum ('*Sea Fort*') which is now Carmarthen – the birthplace of Merlin.

The Celtic Sea Trade

The Demetae were directly connected with a tribe in south-east Ireland called the Brigantes – who were most probably kindred with the Brigantes of northern Britain (named after Brigantia).

The small bay of St Bride's, in the parish of St Bride's.

The church of Saint Bridget (*Sain Ffraid* in Welsh) was built in the 19th century; but it incorporates salvaged structural features from an earlier Norman church.

St Bride window from Saint Bridget's Church,
St Bride's, Pembrokeshire.

Celtic crosses in the churchyard of Saint Bridget's Church.

The earliest recorded evidence for St Bridget's Church dates to the 13th century; but it is possible that its origins date back to the 9th century.

It is strange that such a small and insignificant place should be the namesake of the entirety of St Bride's Bay; especially as the most western reach of St Bride's Bay is St David's (the patron saint of Wales, *and* its most important cathedral) – why isn't called St David's Bay? Was Bride more important?

After the Roman Empire retreated from the British Isles, at the beginning of the 5th century, Irish settlers moved in from southern Ireland – the Brigantes – and the land of the Demetae became, for the most part, an Irish territory (which explains why Geoffrey of Monmouth should record that the bluestones of Stonehenge were brought from Ireland by Merlin; as the bluestones are from nearby Preseli – not far from Merlin's birth-town, Moridunum). This part of Wales eventually became known as Dyfed until after the

Norman invasion when it became known as Pembrokeshire. As the Irish influence was so strong in Dyfed it comes as no surprise that many Ogham-inscribed pillar-stones have been found in the area, at least twenty-two are known of and others are suspected – and they all date to the 5th and 7th centuries; the most dynamic years of the Celtic Church.

A small freshwater stream flows into the small cove of St Bride's, through an arch in a stone wall. The arch was filled in some time ago, maybe to stop livestock from getting through the wall, but the persistent stream still bubbles through – fresh and cold.

The morning following our stay at the Youth Hostel, my friend and I explored the coastal path; south of St Bride's.

A Land of Horses, Choughs, and Dragons

Following the coastal footpath, heading south around the land of St Bride's Castle, was a superb decision to make. The view over St Bride's Bay was truly amazing. One could easily imagine that we had stepped back in time, away from the modern world, and this feeling grew when we came across a small group of horses – grazing freely. Without any trappings upon them the horses looked wild; and although the noble beasts were calm, their presence above these western cliffs exhilarated us. One in particular was a beautiful white horse – and then I remembered that we were in the land of the horse goddess, Rhiannon.

The beautiful white horse, and in the far distance to the right, across the wide expanse of St Bride's Bay, St David's Head.

The land of Dyfed is the setting for the very first branch of *The Mabinogion*; the story of Pwyll, Prince of Dyfed (and Lord of Annwn) – who marries the goddess Rhiannon.

Rhiannon is one of many Celtic sovereignty goddesses, a personification of the spirit of the land itself, whom any would be king has to marry so that the 'king and the land can be one'; which makes all sovereignty goddesses 'the Bride' of course. Just as Brigantia's motif is the omphalos, the Bride is the very heart of the land. Rhiannon then, is the sovereign 'Bride' of the St Bride's area; and her name probably derives from *Rigantona* (Celtic for Great Queen).

It is thought that through Celtic dialects the 'g' and 't' of Rigantona became silent over the passing of time; and thus became 'Ri-an-on'. In a variety of forms there does indeed appear to be a recurring *Rigan* (Queen) pattern in many goddess names (even in Brigantia).

RIGANTONA
BRIGANTIA
RHIANNON
MOR-RIGAN
A-RIAN-RHOD

Remember that with Celtic mythology we have inherited stories from many different tribes and dialects; and all of these divine sovereignty queens are possible Brides of any would be ruler.

Rhiannon is also remembered as having three magical birds, known as the *Adar Rhiannon* (Birds of Rhiannon). It is said that their singing could 'wake the dead and lull the living to sleep'. These otherworldly, psychopomp, after-life, creatures have already been introduced on pages 12-13; they are the three bird constellations of the Summer Triangle - of which there is more information in the Ogham Grove Archive (see pages 213-214). The *Adar Rhiannon* fly along the great celestial river, The Milky Way, during the summer night skies - thus Rhiannon corresponds with the constellation of Cassiopeia sitting upon the centre of The Milky Way, just as Brighid-Brigantia does.

After our southern ramble along the coastal path, on our return to St Bride's, my friend and I decided to be a bit more adventurous and scrambled down towards the cliffs away from the safety of the path. Again, this was a very rewarding thing to do. The cliffs are formed of a red rock and it felt like we were standing on the Red Dragon of Wales itself; and talking of birds we stumbled upon a rare sight.

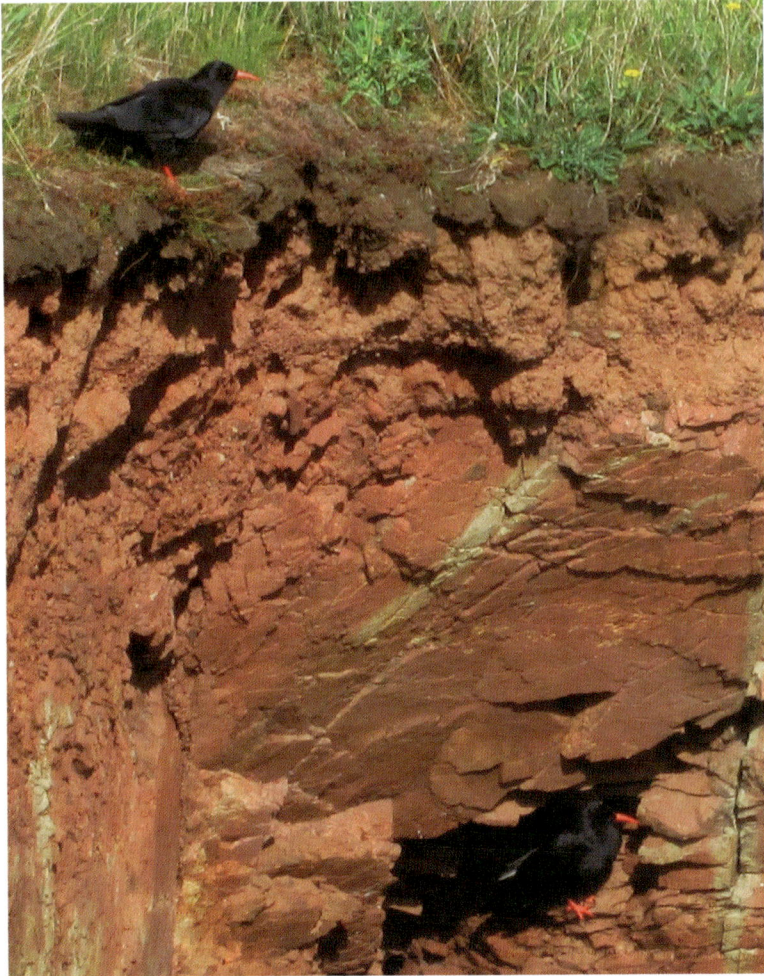

A pair of choughs; members of the crow family, with bright red
beaks and feet – nesting in the cliffs of St Bride's Bay.

Because of the jagged nature of the many promontories of
St Bride's Bay, jutting out into the sea, it is very easy to see
dragons in the shapes of the rocks. The redness of the cliffs
contrasts quite vibrantly, in many places, against the lush
green grass. The following photographs help to capture the
mood and magic of this dramatic landscape.

Dragon scales.

Before leaving, my friend and I took one more look around the small cove of St Bride's. My friend loves looking for special stones and she found a couple of treasures – a small hag-stone of the local red rock, and a lovely grey stone with a profile of the goddess wearing a hood-type head-dress.

Shield of Brighid

By Yuri Leitch

This shield design was inspired by the triple Brigid tradition of
Irish mythology; a swan for each Brigid. A shield because
Brigantia is depicted with one, and Brigid is a goddess of
protection. The three swans are also a nod to the three birds of
Rhiannon, the birds of the Summer Triangle.

~ THE SPIRIT OF BRIGID AND THE FIERY ARROW ~
By Gary Biltcliffe

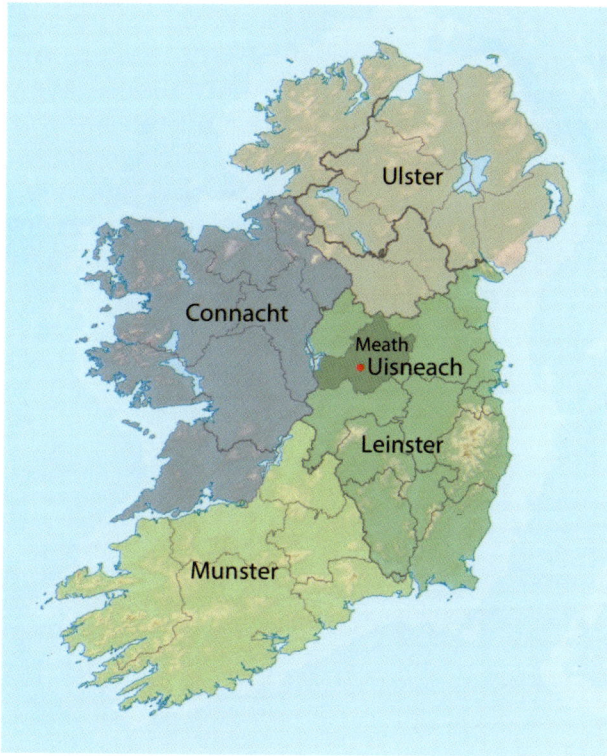

On my first trip to Ireland back in the early 90's, one of the places I most wanted to visit was the Hill of Uisneach, because it was said to be one of the most influential places in Ireland's long and ancient history. Here the first fires were lit in prehistoric times to celebrate the beginning of spring on May 1st, the Celtic festival of Beltane. This initial fire signalled a chain of beacons to light their own celebratory fires across the country to the furthest extremities. It was also said to be the sacred omphalos of all Ireland and the country was divided into four provinces around the hill; which was in a central fifth province called Meath.

Having lost our way driving through the outskirts of Mullingar in the county of Westmeath, on a damp and misty afternoon, I suddenly noticed a small sign pointing to a holy well and I felt a strong pull to visit it. After parking the car, my friend and I followed a muddy footpath to a metal gate. There was not a soul around and as I opened the old rusty iron gate the screech broke the eerie silence over the surrounding fields, and sent a large bird to flight, making us jump. We walked reverently into what appeared to be a graveyard overshadowed by ancient trees in the hedges that seemed to shield the holy place. We followed a winding path marked by tall white-painted standing stones, each one representing a 'Station of the Cross' – a form of Catholic devotion to commemorate the passion of Christ. Suddenly, unusual structures began to emerge from the mist, including a strange beehive mound that covered a holy well and a covered altar area.

Cullion Holy Well of St Brigid

As I wandered around this surreal cemetery, I eventually stopped in front of a life-sized white stone statue of a female saint. I then for some reason instinctively and spontaneously bowed before her and kissed her feet. My friend was rather amused at this, for she had not seen me do anything as reverent as this before, and I had to agree that it was out of character for me at the time. I am not a religious person and rarely visited a church for worship unless it involved a christening, wedding or funeral. I am not an atheist either, having studied many of the world's religions over the years. I found that I resonated particularly with Eastern philosophies including Tibetan Buddhism, for it helps explain the many strange experiences I have had throughout my life.

Feeling a bit foolish, I studied the statue, wondering if it was an old or a particularly special representation of the Virgin Mary. In fact, it turned out to be a modern life-sized sculpture of St Brigid, a saint I was not familiar with at the time, although I knew that she was an ancient Celtic goddess still honoured in Glastonbury. I was mesmerised by the statue that seemed almost life-like in the fading misty afternoon light; but something stirred inside me as if this saint was somehow important and I felt a powerful energy coming from the statue.

Reluctantly leaving Brigid's Well, we headed down the narrow rain-soaked lanes, gingerly avoiding the deep potholes, in search of the Hill of Uisneach. But soon we were lost in the labyrinth of narrow lanes that spread across the middle-lands of Ireland with no sign of an inn or bed and breakfast establishment to rescue us. After driving round and round for what seemed like hours in the now fading light and fog, we stopped and tried to visualise some accommodation. As I concentrated my mind, I saw the large frontage of a white house. We later set off and I drove with an instinctive mindset, turning left or right when I felt the need to do so. We soon found ourselves travelling along a narrow track that appeared to be going nowhere, but then suddenly we spotted a small wooden sign at a junction pointing to a farmhouse B&B. Driving down the winding lane, we were pleased to see a big white house appearing in the headlights just as I had visualised earlier.

A friendly elderly lady answered the door and said she had a room free and invited us in. After sitting us down in front of the log fire, she introduced herself as Ruth and informed me over a restorative cup of tea that the house was in fact built on the site of a monastery. I told her about our frustrating afternoon trying to find the Hill of Uisneach in the mist, and the strange visit to the churchyard, and my initiatory experience with St Brigid. Her reaction rather startled me as she almost jumped out of her chair, exclaiming that 'Well you have found the hill. This house stands at its foot on the site of a Celtic monastery built by St Brigid herself. This land is where she lived!' She pointed to the window at the back and said, 'Out there are the remains of her temple and the water that runs through the taps here comes from her well'. I began to wonder if this was pure coincidence, but then something unusual happened that made me think otherwise.

A family who was already staying there arrived through the front door to break our excited conversation. While they greeted Ruth and seated themselves by the log fire, I walked over to the window, thrilled by the revelation that we were staying on a site sacred to this mysterious St Brigid, and peered into the darkness in the hope that I would see some ruined walls. One of the guests, a young girl about eight years of age, broke free of her parents who were busy chatting to Ruth, and opened the patio door at the back of the house to play in the garden, even though it was dark. At that point I decided to find my room to enjoy a hot bath with water from St Brigid's Well.

Later we arrived back downstairs to a bit of commotion involving the young girl who had been playing outside in the dark. She had run back inside exclaiming to her parents that she had seen a white lady in the garden and pointed to where she had been standing. We all went out to investigate the intruder, but found nobody there. The little girl pointed to a wall saying, 'She stood over there, looking at the house', which Ruth instantly informed us was the ancient wall of Brigid's monastic temple. While the others returned to the house amused at the child's vivid imagination, I lingered for a while by the moss-covered ruined stone wall that appeared to glow slightly in the reflected light coming from the house. As I stood there in the cold night air listening to the trickling water from the well, the cool breeze increased to a gust of wind and suddenly, I felt a strong presence to my right; and through the corner of my eye I caught a glimpse of the shimmering semi-transparent white lady looking at me, but as I turned my head to face the ghostly apparition, there was nothing there but the blackness of the night. I stood for several minutes, hoping to see what I imagined to be the spirit of St

Brigid, but to no avail. Was she trying to communicate with me, and if so, why?

Back inside, Ruth gave me a book on the local history to take up to bed and then said something unsettling. 'You know, ill luck has cursed my lands and all the lands that surround the Hill of Uisneach for hundreds of years.' The book, called *The History of the Diocese of Meath*, revealed the importance of the hill and more importantly, its connection to Brigid. According to the mythology surrounding this hill, the feminine energy within the land was honoured there by successive invaders over thousands of years - in the form of Eriu, Danu, and Brigid; until the arrival of St Patrick who cursed the hill.

UISNEACH

At breakfast the next morning, I sat and pondered whether the bad luck experienced by farmers and businesses around the hill, and the unexplained accidents and deaths, were caused by the curse of St Patrick. Having lived in the area for most of her life, Ruth knew a lot about the history of the hill and its legends, and she kindly offered to take us up the hill after breakfast. Many people believe that every sacred site has its spiritual and physical guardian; if this were true then Ruth was certainly a physical guardian of Uisneach.

As the three of us approached the hill, we passed a sign that read, 'KEEP OUT. THE LAND IS POISONED'. Ruth told us that she was constantly in dispute with the farmer, who did not take kindly to visitors, despite her protests that the hill was then a public right of way. As we continued to trudge around the wet and muddy fields over fences and gates, Ruth's enthusiasm for the site brought the place alive. She introduced us to a mound on the summit where kings were traditionally crowned on an inauguration stone called the 'Stone of Destiny', rocky outcrops where the first Beltane fires were lit, grass ridges that formed the foundations of royal palaces, and watery holes in the ground that were once honoured as the holy wells of saints.

We also visited the small half-dried-up lake named after the god Lugh that supposedly birthed the River Boyne, and Lugh's burial mound. Lugh is the god of light and the solar counterpart of Brigid and is still remembered in the Lothian area of Scotland. St Patrick was the first missionary to attempt to Christianise this national sacred hill in the 5th century and legend says that as he arrived, the sacred ash tree on the hill fell to the ground. Patrick put a curse on the sacred stones of Uisneach and, although there was strong resistance from the local Uí Néill clan, he managed to build a Christian shrine there. His place of worship was known as 'St Patrick's Bed', constructed over an ancient cairn of one of the old gods of Uisneach.

Revd Cogan wrote that a monastery was built at the centre of the 6th-century settlement at Killare, just west of the Hill of Uisneach, founded by St Aedh or Hugh who died there in 588 CE. He also tells that as well as St Aedh's monastery, two other churches were built at Killare, one called Temple Brigid and the other named the Court of St Brigid. One of three wells to St Aedh, St Brigid and St Conran were also recorded as existing there; St Brigid's Well can still be visited today near the crossroads to the south of the hill along from the Uisneach Inn. It seems that Ruth's house must be standing on either the Court or Temple of Brigid next to one of her wells. It may have been here that the Christian St Bridget came and received the veil, and where she lived and worshipped under the shadow of the hill.

In 1111 ACE, Killare was chosen as the meeting place for an important synod that divided Ireland into several diocese which still exist today. Obviously, this was an important event and I believe it was significant that the year 1111 was chosen. The number eleven represents both a gateway and sacrifice, the 11th of November being the festival of Martinmas when animals were sacrificed for the coming winter. It is perhaps no coincidence that an Armistice was signed after the First World War between the Allies and Germany on this day in 1918 ending possibly the greatest sacrifice of all, leaving 17 million men dead, ranking this war among the deadliest conflicts in human history. I also had a sense that it was on this day that the spirit of the goddess was finally banished from the Hill of Uisneach. Perhaps I had a role to play here, as this date happens to be my birth date.

On a high point of the hill is an earthwork enclosure with extensive views over the surrounding countryside, which according to Michael Dames in *Mythic Ireland* is the Uisneach fire temple where the sacred flame was lit at sunrise on Beltane before all others. Dames writes that the shape of the fire enclosure 'forms an architectural image of Eriu, like an incarnate squatting goddess, including her "eye" and "womb" chambers'. Perhaps this was the original fire temple of Brigid who in legend is said to have been born on the hill, supposedly one of three daughters of Dagda all called Brigid. The squat goddess image is also reminiscent of the waters that surround Silbury Hill in the Neolithic complex of Avebury, Wiltshire, when the River Kennet floods in the early spring. Interestingly the sarsen stones in the area of Avebury are locally known as Bridestones. Furthermore, south of Silbury is the Broad Well at Alton Priors, which is said to be the source of the Avon river that flows past the great henge at Durrington and Old Sarum/Salisbury, used to be called Brede Well - derived from the ancient British Goddess.

Uisneach Fire Temple

Brigid, or Bride, was also honoured at wells and springs in Britain, Scotland, and Ireland. To the Christians, the pagan goddess Brigid, or Bride, became the 'devil' and the honouring of the goddess and the spirits of the well was replaced by the act of praying to a statue of Mary, the Holy Virgin, erected next to the wells and springs. Many holy wells disappeared under the high altars of churches and cathedrals, the telluric power amplifying the influence of bishops and kings. For the ancients, as well as appeasing the water spirits, the purity of the water was of utmost importance if the land and its people were to thrive. For if the springs become blocked, contaminated, neglected and forgotten, the magnetic field becomes distorted and out of harmony with the natural frequencies of the Earth; the waters no longer having the life-giving powers to balance the land and maintain health for its people.

Eventually, we arrived at another high point on the western side of the hill and Ruth pointed to a group of rocks called St Patrick's Bed, said to be the remains of a megalithic tomb. It was from here that the saint cursed the land as a result of the Druids' refusal to allow this sacred sanctuary to become a Christian site of worship. Ruth explained that the stones were also thought to be the ruins of St Patrick's Church; that was built to Christianise the hill at a key place of power. The curse made by St Patrick would leave a long-term detrimental stain within the land, and aiming it at such a powerful place would only amplify the effects of that curse as it radiated negative energy across the landscape.

We suggested that the curse could be lifted by speaking aloud the Great Invocation, a world prayer, translated from a Tibetan 'Master of the Wisdom' by Alice Bailey in 1947. As we stood facing north, my friend spoke out loud the words of the first verse of the Great Invocation:

'From the point of light within the mind of God,
let light stream forth into the minds of men,
let light descend on Earth.'

We looked up as the light suddenly dimmed to see heavy dark clouds starting to appear. The second verse began:

'From the point of love within the heart of God,
let love stream forth into the hearts of men,
may Christ return to Earth.'

Precipitously the heavens opened with a clap of thunder and it started to hail. She then shouted the third verse above the noise of the falling hail:

'From the centre where the will of God is known,
let purpose guide the little wills of men,
the purpose which the Masters know and serve.'

By now, the hail was hitting us with such force that I fell to the ground, covering my head. Ruth shouted, 'Stop, you are upsetting the spirits.' The pounding hail also forced her to the ground, pulling her coat over her head for protection. My friend was now whimpering from the pain of being hit by large sharp stones of ice, but, seemingly possessed with the will to continue to the bitter end, she shouted the last verse at the top of her voice:

'From the centre which we call the race of men,
let the plan of love and light work out,
and may it seal the door where evil dwells.
Let light and love and power restore the plan on Earth.'

Incredibly, as she spoke the last words, the clouds rolled by, the hail subsided and silence reigned over us once more.

The ground around us was as white as snow and as I ran towards my friend to see if she was okay, I slipped and fell face down into a muddy pool disguised by the hailstones. As I picked myself up, she turned round to see me covered from head to foot in thick mud resembling some hideous bog monster in a horror movie. She let out a stifled scream but it turned into laughter as we looked at each other's white faces. Ruth cast us a stern look, still upset at us for distressing the spirits, and now we were rolling about laughing. How could we! To this day we are uncertain whether we lifted the curse, but prosperity is starting to trickle in and the present owners of the hill have started to allow visitors (but only on guided tours) to its sacred places and are now building facilities, including toilets, an information room, and a car park. Did the spirit of Brigid communicate with me to facilitate healing at this omphalos site or was there another task to come? Had I missed something?

CROGHAN HILL

Many years later, in 2015, my partner Caroline and I set out upon a quest to discover the ancient importance of geographical omphaloi sites in our book *The Power of Centre*. Returning to the Hill of Uisneach I was immediately drawn to return to the hilltop fire temple above the parking area. Here in the circular enclosure my eyes were taken to a prominent pyramidal hill to the southeast, which I later discovered was Croghan Hill. The same power that drew me to Uisneach was now calling me to visit this eminence and research its history. Although the Hill of Uisneach is the true omphalos site of a combined North and South Ireland, I was fascinated by the curious folk memory that refers to Croghan Hill as Ireland's navel or bellybutton. Although it cannot be said to be the geographical centre of Ireland, it does lie at the centre of the Irish Midlands, once ruled over by the powerful kings of Leinster. The hill stands almost solitary over the fertile flatlands and the great peat bogs that stretch for miles around. It is said that the mythical giants of Ireland were unearthed in this vast area of bogland, including the 'Old Croghan Man', who measured approximately 2 m tall and was believed to have died sometime between 362 and 175 BCE. The hill is associated with *Crochen* the daughter of the sun goddess Etain and the mother of Maebh or Maeve, the goddess queen of the kings of Connacht. The hill was formed from an extinct volcano that erupted billions of years ago out of the Bog of Allen. It is the place of 'the vessel of the Earth goddess' and a site of burial that extends back to the Bronze Age. According to legend, the hill is an entrance to a magic underworld called *Bri Ele*; 'Ele' represents the sun goddess of great beauty. But what really interested me was its strong association with St Brigid.

The Christians regarded Croghan Hill as the birthplace of the 6th century St Brigid, where she took the veil and built a monastery, perhaps indicating that it was a place for the ritual and ceremonial honouring of Imbolc, the festival of fire and Brigid's feast day. Another local myth refers to one of three daughters of Dagda, all called Brigid, who works away in her smithy beneath Croghan Hill, creating beautiful cauldrons. The Ulster Cycle of Irish literature mentions Brigid as the triple goddess who represents the waxing, full, and waning moon in the form of the Maiden, Mother and Crone. Her symbol is the triple sun spiral, each of which represents the closely wound quasi-helical shape of the sun's path over a three-month cycle, also representative of a women's nine-month gestation period. In Christian times, the triple goddess symbol became the triskele found in manuscripts and carved on crosses.

Croghan Hill

On Croghan Hill is a well dedicated to Brigid and another to St Patrick just like on the Hill of Uisneach. According to folklore, as St Patrick climbed the hill, his horse jumped halfway up and hit a stone that immediately sprung into a well, the horse having left a knee print on the stone while drinking its waters. Locals believe that if the stone is taken away it will always return to its rightful place. Every St Patrick's Day, on 17 March, there is a local pilgrimage to the site; where people pray and drink from the holy well. Again, this was originally a site revered by the pagan Druids, where a sacred stone probably stood by the spring, later Christianised by Patrick. Interestingly both Croghan

Hill and Uisneach are associated with the Druids, St Patrick, and Brigid - where she received the veil and built a nunnery. On Croghan Hill we discovered an abandoned graveyard on its eastern slopes, said to be the site of the 5th century Bishop Macaille's church; and St Brigid's first convent. St Macaille of Croghan was a disciple of St Mel. He is said to have assisted in presenting the veil to St Brigid on the hill when he witnessed a flame rising from out of her head. We had encountered St Macaille, also known as Maughold, who was a disciple of St Patrick, on the Isle of Man – a region that marks the centre of the whole of the British Isles and Ireland.

There is no historical evidence to account for the legends of a Christian Brigid here, but the flame rising from her head may be an allegory alluding to ancient fire ceremonies performed here like those on Uisneach. We wondered whether Croghan Hill and Uisneach are dual aspects of the omphalos until we discovered a solar connection between the two hills. The guide at Uisneach told me that Croghan Hill marks the midwinter sunrise viewed from the fire temple. In calendar terms, the winter solstice marks the beginning of the year, an event that the ancients recognised as the rebirth of the sun god emerging from the underworld and fertilising the goddess with solar energy.

KILDARE

Drawing this line on the map, I noticed that if it was extended further towards the southeast it goes straight through Brigid's fire house and the high altar of her cathedral in Kildare, where she became abbess of a nunnery. The fire house is now just a square low-walled enclosure in the graveyard but it was here that Brigid tended a perpetual flame with her nuns. Brigid, or St Bridget, is said to have died here and been buried beneath the high altar of the nunnery church, now the cathedral, until her bones were removed for safety.

According to legend, in 480 CE, St Brigid arrived in Kildare with her nuns and founded the 'Church of the Oak Grove', having erected it under a large sacred oak tree on

Drum Criadh (the 'ridge of clay'). The cathedral we see today is thought to stand over the site of this early church, later renamed *Cill Dara* meaning the 'Church of the Oak' from which we get the modern name Kildare. Here within the fire temple a flame was kept burning perpetually right up until the Reformation in the 16th century. According to the writings of the Norman historian Giraldus Cambrensis in *Topographia Hibernica* (*c.* 1146–1223),

> '[Brigid's fire temple] *is surrounded by a hedge, made of stakes and brushwood, and forming a circle, within which no male can enter; and if anyone should presume to enter, which has been sometimes attempted by rash men, he will not escape the divine vengeance.'*

Brigid's Fire Temple, Kildare.

In the ancient world perpetual fires were tended in temples dedicated to the Roman goddess Vesta and the Greek goddess Hestia.

So great was her fame that soon after Brigid's death in 523 CE, a costly shrine was erected in her honour within a new and larger building. For many centuries Kildare maintained a unique order whereby the abbess ruled over a double community of women and men, and the bishop was subordinate in jurisdiction to the abbess. The foundation flourished from the early 7th century, becoming a centre of learning, attracting pupils from overseas as well as from the sons of the Gaelic Irish nobility. As it grew in importance it also became a significant political and secular centre controlled by the powerful kings of Leinster. In the 7th century, it was described by local monk Cogitosus as once being 'a vast metropolitan' of streets and stone steps. Between the years 835 and 998, the cathedral was devastated by Viking raids no less than sixteen times. The *Annals of Ireland* record that the invaders destroyed the town of Kildare 'with fire and sword' and carried off the shrines of St Brigid and St Conleth. Fortunately, the relics of St Brigid were removed to Downpatrick in Co Down for safety before her shrine was completely destroyed.

In 1993 the flame was re-lit by the Brigidine sisters in Kildare who still tend the flame today at their centre, Solas Bhride. Her cult also continues today at the nearby sacred well about 1.5 km south of the town, where people still receive her blessing by caressing her statue and leaving offerings. The pagan cult of the well, cult of the fire, and cult of the oak, were all ancient rituals evolved from the worship of the old Earth goddess - Bride or Brigid.

Standing at the high altar where St Brigid was first buried, it finally dawned on me what the spirit of Brigid was trying to communicate since calling me to Uisneach all those years ago - that all three sites have a symbolic connection. This solar line connects the mortal Christian Brigid at Kildare with the pagan goddess Brigid at Croghan and Uisneach. From the Hill of Uisneach the winter solstice sun rises over the place she was interred and connects the two places where the pagan goddess was born and the mortal received her veil. Therefore, at the winter solstice sunrise the goddess Brigid is reborn out of the Christian Brigid and initiated to Croghan and Uisneach.

Another connection between the three sites can be perceived with the legendary skills of the three daughters called Brigid; which in Irish mythology are associated with a particular talent or ability. One has the skill of poetry, representing intellect; another is skilled at smithcraft, for creativity; and the other with healing, expressive of fertility.

Uisneach is historically a place of poets or 'Aonachs' who would perform during national assemblies at Beltane; the volcanic Croghan Hill is associated with smithcraft as Brigid had her smithy workshop beneath the hill; and Kildare is a sanctuary of healing; therefore, this midwinter alignment from Uisneach to Kildare incorporates the three aspects of the goddess Brigid - activated when the first rays of the midwinter solstice bathe all three sites, symbolically spreading her tri-part power of fertility, creativity and intellect, across the land from Kildare – the site of healing and fertility to the navel or omphalos at Uisneach where it is spread throughout the whole of the country.

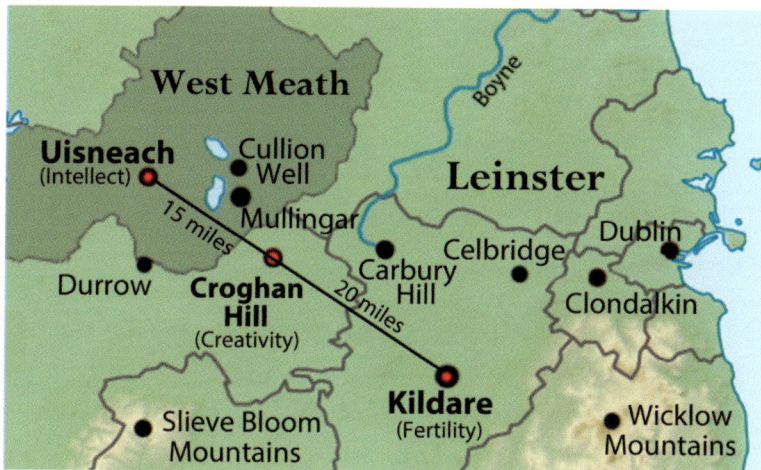

The Three Solar Brigid Sites, or 'Fiery Arrow'.

Keating in *The History of Ireland* suggests the name Brigid is derived from *breo-shaighead*, which means 'arrow of fire' or 'fire of the sun'. Fire is strongly associated with all three sites on this line as it passes through the fire temple at Kildare, where virgins tended the sacred flame; then the fire beacon on Croghan Hill; and then the fire temple on Uisneach, where the first fires were lit to signal all others throughout Ireland.

Perhaps the story of the Christian St Brigid is an allegory of the celebration of this sacred arrow of solar fire, which connects the three aspects of the goddess with the omphalos.

~ CAILLEACH AND BRIDE ~
By Gary Biltcliffe

One allegorical interpretation of Imbolc, on an Earth-Energy level, can be deduced from Gaelic traditions; particularly those of the Outer Hebrides (or Bride's Islands). Here they say that the short spell of good weather that often occurs at the beginning of February is called *'lathan Bridean'* (The Days of Bride).

In the Highlands the Goddess of the land has a dual role, having two personalities - one called Cailleach, who rules over winter – the other Bride, who rules over summer. The Cailleach goes about hammering the land with her great hammer and thus freezing it and creating the frost and snow. During this time Bride is imprisoned by her and kept busy with the impossible task of washing a brown fleece white; but she manages to escape the ordeal on the 1st of February for three days before being recaptured. During her days of escape, far away in the Land of Eternal Youth, Angus Og dreams of the maiden Bride and sets out to rescue her. Eventually Angus Og, with the help of a mysterious male figure (probably the Green Man), locates her and frees her. The Cailleach soon learns of her escape and tries to recapture her, but Bride's release initiates the Spring and this saps the hag's power and energy and she quickly gives up the chase, throwing her hammer under a holly bush. Bride and Angus Og are then married on May 1st and rule together over the Summer months until the winter hag gains her strength and recaptures Bride once more.

The three days of Bride is a release of fertility energy that stirs up the Green Man (energy of rebirth). Therefore, the three days of energy, from the traditional 1st February to the astrological 3rd February, is a window of opportunity to send and receive healing from the land at sacred sites.

The Lady Morgaine
By Yuri Leitch
from the Well Maidens of the Summerlands project

wellmaidens.co.uk

~ AWAKENING THE BRIDE CONSCIOUSNESS ~
IN THE LAND
By Caroline Hoare

The spirit of the goddess Bride has shown herself to me in many forms over the years and one such magical moment was whilst staying on the Holy Island of Lindisfarne, off the east coast of Northumberland. The tidal island is linked to the mainland by a causeway that the North Sea floods for a five-hour period twice a day, depending on the time of year. When the waters recede, visitors make their way to the island across the causeway either by car or walking over the estuary from the mainland guided by wooden marker-poles along the final stretch of the Pilgrims Way from Hexham.

The Holy Island of Lindisfarne

I felt there was a mystical unseen quality about Lindisfarne and I sensed the only way to experience this was to stay on the island. My partner Gary and I were lucky enough to pick a glorious week in May, giving us blue skies and warm temperatures for most of our stay on the island. We rented a small self-catering cottage in the village close to the priory, which historically lies just within the ancient monastic boundary. As soon as we arrived, we were keen to explore the island and its many pathways; and visit the priory ruin and castle. The eerie cooing sounds of the large colony of seal pups in the estuary mixed with the haunting cries of the curlew, seemed to enhance the potent atmosphere of the island.

We eventually found ourselves just a few feet from the shore just beyond the abbey; looking across to a little islet where St Cuthbert is said to have built a cell. To visit it, we had to wait for the tide to recede so we decided to rest on a nearby bench to watch this wonderfully unique phenomenon; when Lindisfarne's causeway suddenly appears allowing the island to become accessible to the mainland once more. Mesmerised by the action of the tide and the wraith-like call of the seal pups, we began to sense that the ebb and flow of the sea as it crashes against the rocks is somehow helping create the island's holy atmosphere.

That night I had a dream that I was being led by a strong female presence across the island, showing me a line of powerful rocks and taking me to certain sacred places including a holy well. When I awoke the next morning, I discovered that Gary had almost the exact same dream. Gary has had dreams before at sacred places that often contain information about the history of the site. He also believes that those who are sensitive can communicate directly or indirectly with the nature consciousness or genius loci of the land, to help us connect with the local energy field, whether it be for healing purposes or to receive specific messages.

Reading further about the island, I realised that one of the places in my dream was St Cuthbert's Isle and the whaleback-shaped hill that overlooks the abbey called the Heugh. Here, we found the scant remains of a stone chapel, which locals believe was the site of the very first island church built by St Aidan; who came from Iona in 635 CE to establish the earliest religious community here. We discovered that St Cuthbert's Isle and the Heugh lie on a geological fault of volcanic dolerite, or black basalt, called Whin Sill that runs east-west through the southern end of the island; also creating the hill upon which Lindisfarne Castle sits. We continued along this line of powerful rocks passing the majestic castle set high above us on a volcanic plug ending at Castle Rocks. We stood by the rocks at the end of our journey wondering what to do next. Had we somehow helped to heal this fault line?

After some time, we headed north along the shore path and soon arrived at a place called Bride's Hole. Here, every year, Whooper swans are said to rest before their migration south. Many cultures referred to Bride or Brigid as the swan goddess and associated her with the worship of the northern constellation of Cygnus. Andrew Collins writes that,

'In Britain, the cult of the swan is likely to have come under the protection of Bride, whose feast day, 1st February, marked the northern departure of the migrating swans.'

At some point in the past, the stork was replaced by the swan as the bringer of new-born babies, perhaps due to Bride's association with fertility.

I then remembered that before I came on this trip, our psychic friend Marie mentioned I had to connect with Bride. Was this sheer coincidence or was the spirit that came into our dreams and guided us across the island to this place, Bride herself?

Whilst sitting at Bride's Hole breathing in the atmosphere, we remembered the holy well seen in our dream. We consulted our local map of the island, and there in very small script was a dot and the name *Bridge Well* also known as *Brig Well,* located in the middle of the island. As we approached the well, Gary suddenly sensed a presence of a powerful energy coming from a field enclosed by a dried-stone wall. As we looked over the wall, we noticed it was filled with wild chamomile. The energy was soft and feminine and gave us a tingling sensation. We lingered for a while smelling the gentle fragrance of the wild herb wondering why this place felt so special.

Nearby at the meeting of two tracks, we suddenly heard the sound of trickling water. As we drew closer, we suddenly saw a mound in the grass with a stone lintel across an opening. Although the belief is that the well was named after the King's Bridge that once stood in the vicinity up until the 17th century, we also knew that Brig was another name for Bride; also referred by the earliest tribes of Britain as Brid or Brigid, who represents the intelligence of nature, fertility and the element of fire.

Bridge or Brig Well, Lindisfarne

Sadly, it was overgrown and neglected and we felt it needed honouring in some way. So we cleared away the mouth of the well, of its overgrown vegetation, and picked one of our sacred stones; which I immediately recognised as a serpentine stone from Iona, which holds the very essence of mother earth and her nourishing healing power. We placed the stone in the well and spoke the following well-blessing; inspired by Lunaea Weatherstone in *Tending Brigid's Flame*,

'May these waters be filled with power, light and grace.
As with Brigid's holy well in Kildare,
So shall it be in the waters of this land.
May all who touch these waters be filled with healing
For mind, body, and spirit.
May the waters of this well be filled with the blessings
Of the goddess Bride.
By the power of earth, air, fire and water,
I dedicate this well to Bride.
May her loving energy bless and preserve us
With her healing, protection, and grace.
As I will it, so shall it be!'

After the ceremony we took away the stone, having transferred its healing power to the well, and we returned to our cottage believing we had succeeded in our task.

However, the next day we woke up early in the morning having had the same dream again, but this time we were dowsing the line of rocks with our angle-rods. We again returned to St Cuthbert's Isle where the fault of basalt rocks goes out into the bay across to the mainland. This time we sensed and dowsed a feminine earth energy line passing through the remains of St Cuthbert's Cell. It avoided the Heugh and instead headed north to the parish church dedicated to St Aidan; its foundations dating from Saxon times. In the graveyard to the church, the female energy line passes through an ancient stone sockct called the Petting Stone. According to an old island tradition, any new bride married in the church had to be assisted over the stone by the island's fishermen. The tradition has spanned generations and is said to bring good luck and fertility to the newlyweds. Every girl on her wedding day adopts the name 'Bride' - for symbolically and unconsciously she takes on the role of the great mother-goddess, whose purpose is to generate fertility to bring life into the world and to keep the fires burning in the hearth. The line then continued through the Norman priory and then re-joined the Whin Sill line of rocks in the harbour; and across to the castle and Castle Rocks.

At the time, we were unaware that this was to be the beginning of a new adventure - following a male and female earth energy alignment along a straight axis across Northumberland and Scotland, and finally to the Hebrides (Bride's Isles) and the island of Iona; whose stones we used to heal the well. Along the way, this female spirit guided us to many glorious sites, including cup and ring marked rocks, hermit caves, and a hillfort within the wild bleak landscape of Doddington Moor. Here, across this vast moorland, we became lost trying to trace the female current that we now called Bride. Suddenly, we saw in front of us an adder basking in the warmth of the sunshine. It immediately raised its head and hissed and then slithered away under the gorse. Bride, as the goddess of birth and fertility, has her animal consorts which includes the swan, the cow, and in Scotland and Northern England the adder. Amazingly it was here we picked up the feminine energy line to the hillfort.

THE FIRE GODDESS OF THE OMPHALOS

Britain has an element of this ancient goddess in its name. The Greek geographer and explorer Pytheas, when visiting the British Isles in 325 BCE, called them the *Pretannikē* Islands. According to Strabo, the name Pretannikē is Greek for the island of Pretan or Pretani. Linguists believe this to be a Celtic word meaning 'the painted ones' or 'the tattooed folk', observed later by the Roman general Julius Caesar.

Around 100 BCE a great change took place in the languages of northern Europe whereby a great many words that had previously contained the sound of the letter 'P' changed to the sound of 'B' and likewise 'T' to 'D', a concept known today as Grimm's Law. Therefore, Pretani sounds like Bredani, a derivative of Bredy, Brid, Bride, Brit, Brigantia and Britannia.

Remarkably similar to Britannia is the goddess Barati, depicted on Phoenician coins with her fire cross set in the throne. The Phoenicians were a mysterious race of seafaring nomads who traded around the Mediterranean for over 5000 years and, according to early writers and local archaeological evidence, they often visited Britain. Barati is said to be the European equivalent of Brita and Bride, an Aryan Phoenician title that may originate in ancient India. Her original sacred places, particularly in Ireland, Scotland and Northern Britain, still exist, although many are Christianised as St Bridget shrines and some still lie hidden awaiting discovery.

The Celtic Brigid or Bride, whose Christian counterpart is named St Bridget, is connected to many centre-places both in the land and in the home, where she is protector of the hearth. In the round houses of indigenous tribes around the world, past and present, the hearth is at the centre of the home and a source of warmth, comfort and nourishment around which they gather. The central pole that holds up the roof or the chain that suspends the cauldron is the symbolic axis mundi, our link between heaven and earth - the hearthstone representing the body of our world.

VESTA.

The Greek Island of Delos was deemed to be the cult centre of Apollo and an omphalos where the perpetual flame resided, but was also the abode for the followers of the moon goddess Brizo, protector of women. She was seen as an oracle who could predict the success of fishing expeditions. Robert Graves in *The White Goddess* believes that Brizo may have been the Aegean prototype of Brigid. The Romans had an equivalent deity in Vesta, the virgin goddess of the hearth, whose centrally-located temples held a perpetual flame tended by pure women known as Vestal Virgins. Roman writer Dionysius of Halicarnassus wrote,

'And they regard the sacred fire as consecrated to Vesta, because that goddess, being the Earth and occupying the central position in the Universe, kindles the celestial fires from herself.'

The worship of Vesta ended in 394 CE when Christian emperor Theodosius I closed the temples; prohibiting the worship of all pagan gods. Her origins appear to be Trojan, stemming from the legendary migrants under Aeneas who founded the city of Lavinium, on the coast east of Rome; which housed the first temple to Vesta in Italy.

Vesta, was the virgin goddess of the hearth and in Greece, she was Hestia, one of the twelve Olympian deities. Like the Celtic Brigid of Ireland, she was also one of three virgin goddesses.

The 5th century Christian St Brigid had her main sanctuary at Kildare, where she guarded a perpetual flame along with nineteen virgin maidens during a 20-day cycle.

Her flame was honoured at every hearth in every home and at the smithy, whose fires create the utensils and tools of life and death. A statue of her at a nearby holy well on the outskirts of Kildare is remarkably similar to Vesta.

During the long-term settlement of the Saxon tribes in Britain, compartmented rectangular or square dwellings appeared, making communal living in easy-to-build round houses redundant. This new way of constructing homes led to the relocation of the hearth from the centre of the home to the outer wall of the main living room, although it remained the focal point of the house. Today, the mantelshelf over the fire serves as a symbolic altar on which we place our precious objects, with the hearthstone symbolic of the Earth.

The Fire Goddess, St Brigid of Kildare.

Bride and the Earth Serpent

I was first introduced to the many Bride sites in the north while investigating the Belinus alignment for our book *The Spine of Albion*. Along this north-south line, Gary and I followed two earth energy dragons, one yang/male and the other yin/female, similar to the Michael and Mary lines dowsed by Hamish Miller. This long-distance alignment forms the longest through-route from the Isle of Wight at the southern base of Britain to the northern tip of Scotland near Durness; connecting Winchester, the old capital of England, with the old Scottish capital of Dunfermline. In fact, it connects six cities in all, including Carlisle, the old Roman capital of the north; Manchester and Birmingham, the industrial capitals of the 19th and early 20th centuries; and Inverness, the capital of the Highlands. Our journey along the spine of Britain took us to several lost religious and historical places of ancient significance, on both the currents and alignment; their mystery enhanced with thrilling legends and folklore.

The Bridestones monument, located in the saddle of an enigmatic hill called The Cloud, on the borders of Staffordshire and Cheshire, is one such example. It consists of a group of standing megaliths, which is all that remains of a Neolithic long barrow dating from 3500 BCE. It sits next to Dial Road, which derives from 'deiseal' (*deas* being the Celtic word for the right hand and *sul* meaning the sun). This refers to a very ancient ceremony of walking three times around a stone circle east–west, depending on the course of the sun, their right hand pointing towards the centre as the ancient priests circled the stones; walking in the opposite direction is termed 'widdershins'. Perhaps it was a place to honour Bride as the goddess of fertility and regeneration, and to harness the life-giving qualities of the feminine earth dragon, thus inducing spiritual harmony and aiding fertility within the land. Before leaving this sacred sanctuary of Bride, we said the following words,

May the goddess Bride bless this land and its people.
May the encompassing of Bride protect you.
May the encircling of Bride cherish and sustain you.
May the soft hand of Bride soothe you
and give you strength.
May the eye of Bride keep watch over you
and show you the way.
May the heart of Bride love you
and provide you with health and well-being.
Be with us on this day and everyday.

The Bridestones monument.

Another mystical site of the fertility goddess, and the Belinus Line feminine earth serpent, is St Bride's Kirk; which lies at the geographical centre of Scotland within the grounds of Blair Castle; owned by the powerful Dukes of Atholl. The old kirk sits on a sacred mound, a remnant of a time when the Picts created a shrine here in honour of their goddess Bride. The Picts revered the goddess spirit of the land and knew how to benefit from her healing and rejuvenating energy; and in particular the feminine serpent energy. Despite their war-like reputation, the Picts had a sacred relationship with all elements including plants, animals, and stones. They felt part of nature and not separate from it, regarding everything as an extension of the Universe. According to the folklorist Stuart McHardy,

'Their rituals were a celebration of the unfolding of creation itself and the extraordinary spiritual vitality and sacredness of life. They had the freedom of spiritual expression, honouring and revering nature spirits rather than worshipping divinity'.

As we crossed the threshold of this ancient church, we noticed a cup-marked stone and part of a larger megalith placed in the footings of the north wall, perhaps indications of this site's antiquity. According to folklore, the original and more ancient purpose of these cup and ring marked stones slab was for ritual ceremonial use during certain times of year; such as Imbolc and Beltane. The marks were made by quartz stones ground sun-wise into the slab, which may have had a positive and curative effect upon the landscape to help with the fertility and well-being of the land.

We have found evidence of Bride sanctuaries at other geographical central places including Wales, Ireland and the Isle of Man; detailed in our book *The Power of Centre*. This left me in no doubt that St Bride's Kirk was once an important cult centre of this fertility goddess. Before we left, we said a blessing,

May the goddess Bride bless this naval of Scotland
and its people.
May the encompassing of Bride protect us.
May the encircling of Bride cherish and sustain us.
May the soft hand of Bride soothe us and give us strength.
May the eye of Bride keep watch over and show us the way.
May the heart of Bride love us
and provide us with health and well-being,
Be with us on this day and everyday.

The Great Mother in the form of Bride or Brigid and her sacred flame represents the flame or light within us, the spiritual energy that ignites our soul at the core of our being and all things. She is the protector at the hearth of our home, goddess of fertility and sovereignty. By connecting with her at her special places in the landscape, I found I was able to recapture, at a heart-level, the goddess energy within me.

For further information about Gary Biltcliffe and Caroline Hoare, and their ongoing investigations into sacred sites and the energies of the land, you can visit their website and Facebook group,

www.belinusline.com

Facebook – **The Spine of Albion**

Book One of The Chronicles of Ogus

A Chlann An T-Soluis
The Children of Light

I am very proud and happy to announce this soon to be published book; written by my father, Ian Leitch, and illustrated by myself. It is a large hardback of 280 pages, and it includes twenty full-page illustrations, one for each of the trees in the Ogham – the picture on the opposite page (and those on pages 26 and 167) are three of the twenty.

The Chronicles of Ogus tell the epic story of an immortal life, journeying through century after century, in both this mortal realm and in the Celtic Otherworld.

Book One follows Ogus, a neolithic flint-flaker, as he transitions from the life of a mortal human into living the eternal existence of a sidhe – a spirit of Light. His journey takes him across the River Severn, through Wales, the Isle of Man, and the western isles of Scotland, to Orkney; and then, via sidhe-flight, to many other places.

Accompanied by his faithful wolf companion, Ogus visits sacred site after sacred site (real places that can still be visited to this very day), following a swirling transformative adventure in which he encounters many gods, goddesses, and heroes of Celtic mythology – learning the wisdom of the Ogham along the way.

The following prose is the preface to Book One. For further information please join the Facebook group – The Chronicles of Ogus – or my website **www.yurileitch.co.uk**

And we are here, yet you do not see us.
We have always been here, descendants of Nemed,
Unchanging; of no age and every age.

Men, a loose term for fools and apes,
Swept us hither and thither,
So we went to ground, keeping to ourselves.

Fir Bolg, Fomoraig, flint-flakers.
Men, when they had the foresight to become farmers,
Came close to us,
Their hounds came closer.
Hounds still are aware of us,
Their senses closer to reality than those of men.

In the days of Ossian, Taliesin and Finnegas,
The days of Fionn Mac Cumhail and his followers,
Now sleeping with the three sisters.
When the melodious cave
First echoed the music of willow and rowan,
The string of a harp.

Aileen of the fire words
Sowing the seeds of the reed calendar.
Bardic sorcery told silent tales of the sixth day of the moon,
The mistletoe of Duir.
The men in white with the knowledge of the salmon,
Gaining sight of Iona,
The last haven of the kings;
Watching Dis as he claimed his rights.

We who had moved to great Orkney,
Teaching the farmers to build.
Listening to the words of Celts and Vikings;
The sword in fist,
The shield in battle.
Fierce boats steered by heroes
And non-existent gods.

Why do men need gods when we have always been here?

The constant veil twixt worlds
Is finer as cattle come in from the chill.

Samhain, festival of harvest, home, and death.
Festival of the passing into dark

From the light part of the year,
Cattle to be driven between fires to the byre.
Great divination, dreams foretold and other insights,
Casting lots for future knowledge, first written in the stars.
Dowsing with witches rods, hazel witch hazel, and osier.
The time of seers and oracles,
The newness of the newest year.
Born of the old decay.

Half open doorway to the sidhe;
The veil between worlds thinned to the finest spider gauze.
The birth of Blodeuwedd, fairest of women born of twigs,
Meadowsweet, oak and broom, wife of Llew, faithless owl,
Cursed to live by night, damned to hunt the evening hawk.
Rhiannon riding the uncatchable white steed,
Clothed as a goddess in gold,
Queen goddess cursed by lies of infanticide;
Clearer of Mab's magic mist.

When the hawthorn blooms, Beltaine,
The yellow day breaks as dawn.
The day of cleansing fire,
The time of thrusting fertility.
The days of longer sunshine
Shorten the night and moon mist,
A lusty time when **we** have always done our best work.

Thus in a time of men the Milesians went to Eire
And drove out the sacred Tuatha Dé Danann,
The followers of Danu, of heaven and earth.
Lugh and Midir, warriors both,
Sailed past the blessed islands
Back to the glen of Ossian's birth,
The weeping glen, to the cairns of the sidhe.
There they met Manannan mac Lyr;
He who led them to other earth, to live for Millennia.

Éadaoin the twice born butterfly

Rode Enbarr of the flowing mane
To the same glen.
There to reunite with Midir, the swans enjoined again.
Enbarr, as faithful as the best of hounds,
Grazed the heather,
White of purity, purple of honour,
Leaving the sour leaves to winter,
Cheating the bees.

The Time of men does not exist with us within our cairns.
Here in the light of extreme beauty,
The land of Mab, Oberon, Titania, and Merope,
The land where conjurers and magicians
Have one foot in mystery,

Imbolc, herald of spring,
Searching for badgers and serpents;
To declare among the snowdrops, blackthorn,
And imprints in shallow snow.
Nature in pregnant pose,
Aware of lactation performed by waiting ewes.
Man reliant on wicks and fire, light and warmth,
Unfolding the family from hovel and roundhouse.
Fires lit in glades and heath,
Cremating the old growth,
Purifying for the new,
Cailleachann gathering kindling.
Biera, queen of winter, deer herder,
Losing her grip for a while.
Bonfires celebrating rebirth,
Gazing for omens,
Witnessing the stars.

As the days lengthen, the white plaid restored.
Mistletoe berries taken for food by birds,
Mistle Thrush seeking new boughs.
Acorns and hazel nuts stir in their cases
Nuzzling into mother earth.

Creatures waken from dreamscapes,
Ready to hustle-bustle in hedgerows.
Hounds stretch limbs ready for the season of the hunt.

We, the people of the hollow mountain,
Beinn Cruachan, maintain watch,
Rejuvenating our youth,
Just as nature,
For eternity.

The land of magic and things unknown to mankind,
Unseen to witless eyes.

Lughnasadh, early harvest, the day of sacrifice.
The old bull makes way for the yearling bull.
Lugh making the funeral speech for his foster mother,
Now carving the old beef.
Folk gathering bilberries or dressing wells
As sacred as time.

Tailtiu baker of the first Lunastain cake
Giving strange credence to Carmun,
Warrior sorcerer from her ancient Greek homeland,
Plain clearer.
Lightening stone thrust towards Lugus the wave-sweeper,
The yew spear and faithful Failnis,
Baying at the sacred ball of fire
As it rises, mellow, in the morn.
Below the sentinels, cairns and megaliths,
(some in inaccessible places),
Labyrinths of stone and sacred trees,
Guarded by wolves and sidhe.

We, who corral and husband the ponies
With dripping manes.
What know you of nuggles and kelpies?
Beathac Mor, Morag or Sailleag?

All are seen and not seen,
Yet they exist.

Our names are many:
Beith, Luis, Fearn, Saille, Nion,
Uatha, Duir, Tinne, Coll and Quert.
Muin, Gort, Ngetal, Straif, Ruis,
Ailm, Onn, Ur, Eadhadh and Idho.

Trees and shrubs and letters,
We leave you our magic lines.

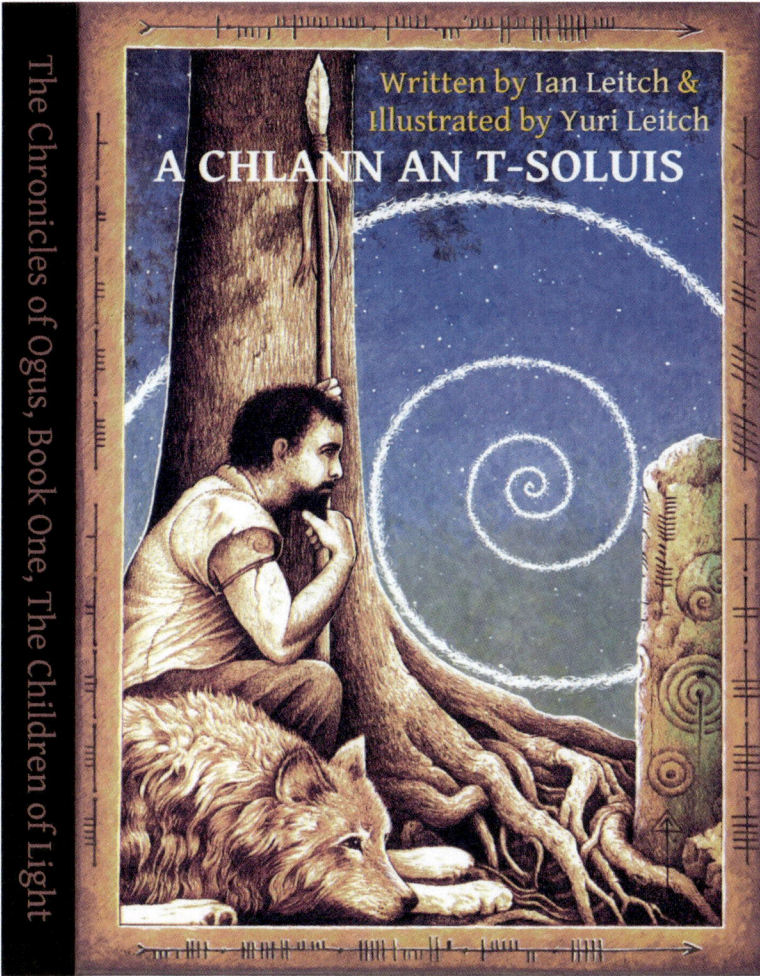

Written by Ian Leitch &
Illustrated by Yuri Leitch

A CHLANN AN T-SOLUIS

The Chronicles of Ogus, Book One, The Children of Light

~ COMING SOON ~
(Summer 2021)

The shield and spear are
The circumference
And the vertical axis
To the omphalos
And the centre of being.

MEMBERS GALLERY

ART & PROSE

~ NAOMI CORNOCK ~
Artist

I have awarded Naomi's picture, the *Three Faces of Brigid* for the following reasons:

Whilst she has skillfully interwoven the three aspects of the triple Brigid of Irish tradition (healer, smith, and poet), I have awarded her the Hawthorn Stake for my favourite artwork because she has captured something of the Celtic matriarchal protective warrior goddess. A lot of Brighid artwork is influenced by the pure and holy (meek and mild) Saint Bridget of Kildare – and there is nothing wrong with that, it is a spiritual ideal – but Naomi's Brigid carries an essence of the 'spear and shield' of Brigantia, the great *Magna Mater* that will fight, if need be, to protect her young.

Three Faces of Brigid

by Naomi Cornock ©

Winner of the award for the Editor's favourite artwork
contribution.

Brigid's Song

by Naomi Cornock ©

Naomi Cornock is a very prolific pagan artist, and she has created a mass of inspirational artwork; please check out her web pages for more of her work,

www.nomeart.com
Instagram ~ **Naomi Cornock**
Facebook ~ **nomeartuk**

Rowan

by Naomi Cornock ©

~ ANNIE LOUVAINE ~
Artist & Poet

Imbolc, The Maiden Awakens

by Annie Louvaine ©

Annie's websites
www.redbubble.com/people/wildwoodgroves
www.etsy/uk/shop/thewildwoodsofavalon
www.fineartamerica.com/profiles/1-annie-clark

An Ode to Brigid – Protector of Albion

On ancient earth my feet hold firm and steadfast,
Rooted deeply through the layers of Eternal Dust.
Attuned and resonant to Albion's beating Heart,
I migrate along Her Enchanted Pathways.
Her silver threads glisten and call in the moonlight,
As they weave their song around the dragon's fiery breath.
Tracking this time-worn land, through forests,
Moors and mountains,
The cries of Curlew, Owl and Wolf alert my senses.
Fine-tuning me to the very essence of her Great Being.

Tempest winds sculpt and bend the terrain to their icy blasts,
The wild squall echo with the voices of my Ancestors.
I lend my ear as they sing their dreams within my Soul.
These ancient lands are soaked with the blood of my kin,
This soil bears their joys and woes of bygone ages.
Their bones and prayers make fertile this sacred ground,
From which all life births and springs forth in an endless spiral.
Her Breath and Waters are our breathe and waters,
Her Fire is our fire, forever burning bright to light the way.

Behold the Great White Goddess! Brigid of Albion.
Breo-saigit, Sovereign Swan, Great Mother Guardian,
Protector, Healer and Weaver of our Lineage of Clans.
She expels Her arrows of Divine Fire through rarefied Air.
She stands guard over the Holy Well Springs of Pure Waters.
She spins sacred poetry to anoint these Isles with Her Glory.
Adorned with cinquefoil foliage holding nurture for all our woes,
She holds the Holy Grail aloft, for all that are worthy to seek.
It is Her Vital Force pulsing through our veins,
Flesh and land as one.

by
Annie Louvaine

Rowan Luis Mandala

by Annie Louvaine ©

Annie writes ~ I am deeply connected to the land; I grew up on a small holding in the 1970's in a place called Rosedale which is in the heart of the North York Moors National Park. This was a time before we were over-run by the volume of traffic we have now, and before the tourist industry took off. I was a very solitary child (no siblings) and in a very small population (only eighteen children in the whole school, infant/junior, and only five of us in my class). My parents were always very busy, so the land was my parent.

I had a number of special places where I would spend a lot of time. I knew exactly where different types of wildflowers would grow and could sense the energy in different places. Some places I explored would have very dark, dangerous energies, and I would avoid those. Others were light and full of Fae energy - and they were my playground. I would spend hours exploring and sitting in hideaways I had found amongst the overgrowth of Hawthorn, Broom, and Gorse; which grew alongside the hillside Springs. Or I would be on the moors amongst the heather and the moor bogs and ponds. There were lots of woodland areas and a tree-lined stream (River Seven) that ran along the valley base which I explored in great detail. I was so fortunate to have had these childhood experiences with the land and nature and it has formed and shaped the core of who I am in this life. It's my greatest comfort and of course, it's where we find the doorways to Spirit and All That Is.

Annie also manages these two Facebook pages
www.facebook.com/wildwoodgroves
www.facebook.com/wildewoodsofavalon

* * *

Flamekeeper's Prayer

May we encounter Brighid in our darkness.
May Her bright beauty enthrall us,
Her warm sparkling gaze enchant us,
Her healing waters engulf us,
Her protection thrice encircle us,
Her soft mantle enfold us,
Her infinite pantry supply us,
Her Imbas enlighten us,
Her call for justice energize us,
Her fiery passion empower us.
May Brighid's ancient, enduring presence daily engage us,
And we shall burn bright,
Enflamed by Her.

by Bridee Redbud
Flamekeeper, Clann Bhride

The Sacred Grove

by Ina Whistler ©

Brigid the Goddess of Light

by Ina Whistler ©

Ina writes ~ I wanted to add a little bit about myself, my work and practices, and how both are strongly linked to who I am, and why I connected so strongly with The Ogham Grove.

I am a practicing Green Witch, I'm super intuitive to energy, and I love working with crystals and herbal medicine in my spare time; but mainly I'm an artist and writer - and I love the connection I have to the natural world, which can also be found throughout my work.

I come from a long line of Roma women, and Celtic men, but didn't know this until about seven years ago. My mum passed away and I inherited a box of what I now call my magic - a spell book/diary, some tarot cards, a pendulum, a crystal angel, and some other stuff related to my mum, Nan, and Glastonbury; and their practice which I'm saving for another time.

All of these things have lead me on a path which has been the most rewarding, it's also lead me down a rabbit hole and to a life I could have only imagined, but it is and has been a integral part of who I am now; and a journey I know is my own - and I love that so much - it has given me peace and understanding and it has made me deal with my shadow.

Even though looking back there are plenty of times - I can now understand why my Nan put water out for the moon, or why my mum put salt on windowsills every time we moved house, or why I had a dream catcher above my bed to ward of bad dreams, or why my Nan would read tea leaves and palms, and use a pendulum to determine the sex of a pregnant aunt's baby, or why my mum had a herbal cure for everything, and horse shoes hung in the garden, and a bell and old keys by the front door. Now I understand, and I understand why they kept it from me; which is another story in its self I hope to one day share.

But since finding Yuri's work on the Ogham lore and trusting it's ways I've actually learnt so much about myself; about my patience, and practice, about letting what comes flow, and learning to let go of needing to control, and connecting back to nature and my shamanic roots has been the best medicine I could have asked for.

The prose I have written this time are writings that I have done whilst I've been out in the woods, sat with what I call my talking trees - these three trees are a Rowan, a mighty old Oak, and a Silver Birch. I often visit these trees, but last summer I decided to sit and meditate under the old mighty Oak and see what would come up for me, and I was gifted with a wolf guide who now shows up every time I meditate to lead the way - I think it's related to my mum because she loves wolfs and white ones especially, which is what my guide is, he's loving and protective.

Incantation for St Brigid

I call upon you St Brigid, keeper of the light.
Teacher of the Ogham lore.
Guide me into your heart, guide me with your eternal flame.
Keep me safe, keep me warm
Bring with you a new day
Bring me a new dawn.
May your light guide the way,
I walk your path I call your name,
Brigid the guardian of all things bright
And light and grown,
Watch over our hearths and homes.
Healer of the heart
Mother of this waking land
I call your name.
Brigid the guardian of the land
Of all things bright
And light and grown.
I stand here in your Ogham grove
Your light guides me to my ancestors and takes me home.
For you are St Brigid, keeper of the veil,
Holder of the flame,
Thank you for your blessings,
Thank you for the flame that burns bright,
Thank you for your eternal light.

St Brigid Blessed be.

by Ina Whistler

The Sacred Grove

I follow the paths my ancestors told;
It takes me to a sacred place,
A magical sacred grove.

The Sun dances in the trees,
Making a kaleidoscope of jewelled greens and yellows
That dance upon the floor.
The smell of abundance is everywhere.
I hear the bird song high in the trees.
I can hear the scurrying of small creatures all around me.

Buzzing bees, busy with their day,
I follow my path and continue on my way.
I can hear the beating of my heart,
Starting to slow, I rest my breath,
Breathing deep into my soul,
Following the signs that guide me home.

I'm protected and calm,
Safe to go inwards
And carry on,
My journey has only just begun,
I'm surrounded by my Ogham grove,
Kindred spirits of my soul,

Time standing still,
I'm happy, I'm safe, I'm loved.
My kindred spirits hold my hand,
Leading me through the magic veil,
Showing me twenty trees standing tall,
They encircle me and hold me strong,
The Ogham grove guiding me to connect
And learn the sacred way of the Ogham lore.

by Ina Whistler

www.ibwhistlerart.co.uk
Facebook – I.B.Whistler Artist & Illustrator

~ ALAN OUTTEN ~
Designer and Artist

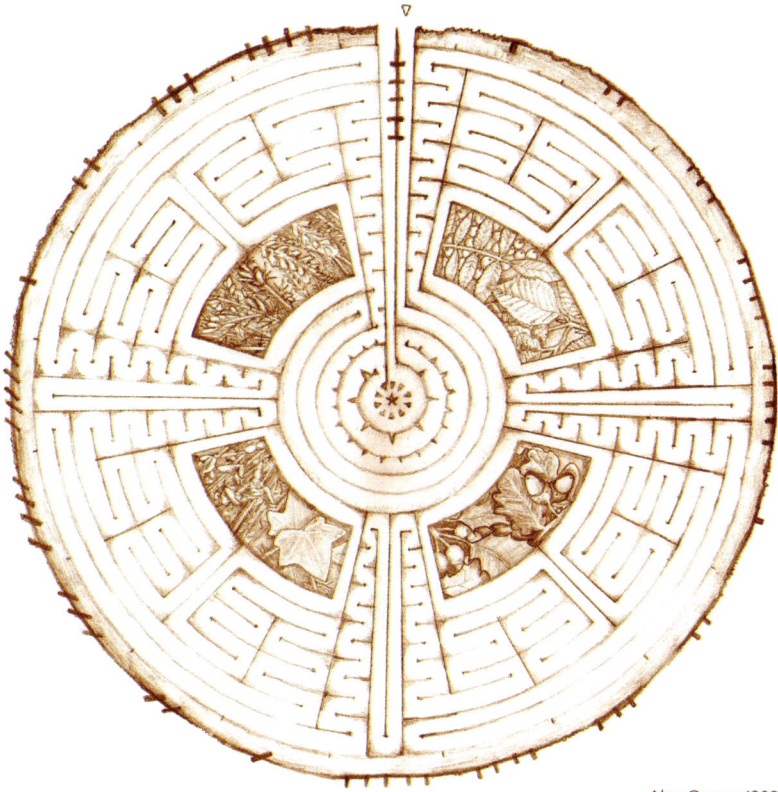

Alan Outten (2021)

Ogham Labyrinth
by Alan Outten ©

Just as the light of the Winter Solstice sunrise enters many ancient sacred sites, like Newgrange in Ireland, I particularly loved that Alan used the Winter Solstice position as the entry-point into his brilliant labyrinth design – totally inspired.

Alan writes ~ The 'Ogham Labyrinth' is part of a personal project looking at ways we might map our individual journeys through the days of the year.

Aiming for something more circular in nature (rather than the more common rectangular layouts we generally find in calendars nowadays) some of my early sketches quickly started to resemble both tree rings and also the classical labyrinth images found in antiquity. These 'unicursal maze' patterns have previously been used both in group ritual and for private meditation and, increasingly, for therapeutic use in hospitals and hospices.

This particular design incorporates elements of the Ogham tree calendar including the four aicme and the twenty trees as well as the eight 'Wheel of the Year' festivals.

Start from the top (the first light after the Winter Solstice) and work your way around the year passing the quarter and cross-quarter days. The latter are represented by the four panels with the corresponding trees (Rowan and Alder for Imbolc, Oak and Holly for Beltane, Ivy and Broom for Lughnasadh and Gorse and Heather for Samhain).

* * *

On the opposite page is Alan's beautifully clear design of the Ogham Year Wheel. It is full of precise details that cannot really be seen very clearly in the format of this book (get your magnifying glass out) – I think it would be great if Alan produces it as a large poster one day.

Alan is a designer and artist based in London, working in areas including architecture, user experience, game and digital design. Please visit his website,

www.alanoutten.com

Of his Ogham Year Wheel **Alan writes** ~ This chart is another part of my personal project; looking at ways to map our individual journeys through the days of the year.

The 'Ogham Year Wheel' shows a number of celestial events through the year. The main event is the journey of the Earth around the Sun. This journey takes slightly longer than a non-leap year to complete (365.25 days) but is exactly 360 degrees. As the Earth's journey around the Sun isn't a perfect circle (it's very near to it though), the timings are a bit trickier to work out. Reading the chart like a clock, the (Gregorian Calendar) year starts a few minutes after midnight.

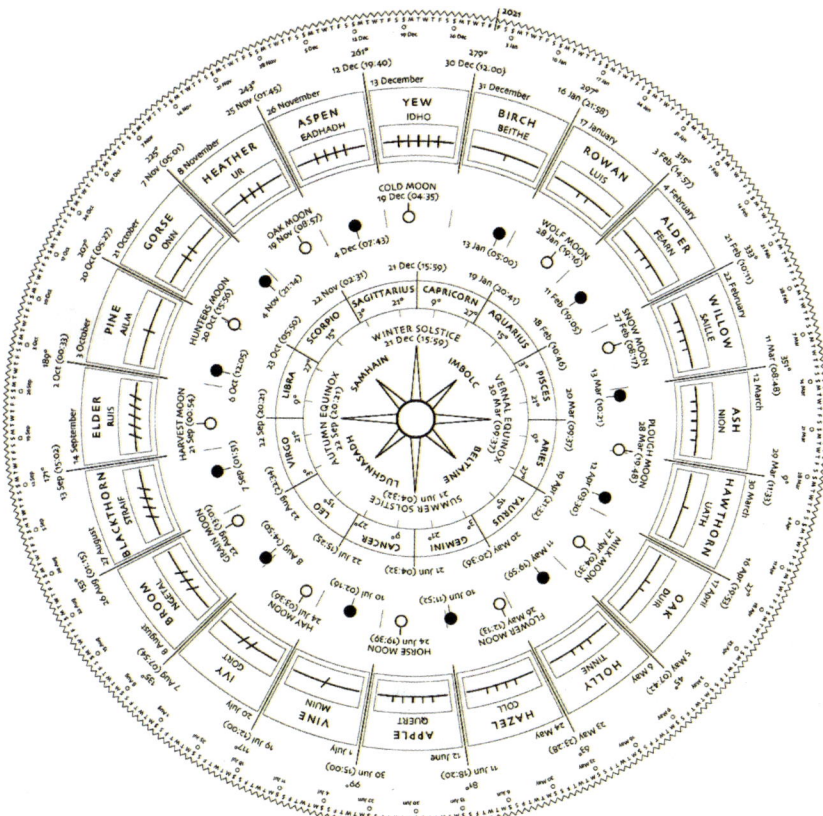

The Ogham Year Wheel
by Alan Outten ©

The Zodiac Signs in the middle of the chart are all spread out evenly at an 'hour' apart (but, again, due to the slightly squished journey of the Earth, some take slightly longer or shorter than others to complete; with the Signs nearer '12 O'Clock' being the shortest as the Earth moves through Space faster at this time of the year as it is slightly nearer to the Sun). Similarly, the twenty 'Tree Days' are evenly spread out (18 degrees each rather than 30 for the Zodiac Signs - 18 x 20 = 360 degrees).

Astronomically, we tend to use the Spring Equinox (Northern Hemisphere) as the starting point for measuring the angle (so Zero degrees and 360 degrees both happen at this point). This aligns with the start of Aries. Normally, we read the angle as an observer on Earth (or, in this case, as an observer in the centre of the Earth - aka, geocentric) looking at where the Sun is in relation to the stars of the night sky (which are pretty much static). The chart gives the dates and times for the Sun (really it's the Earth) to travel through the various angles of the 'night sky' during the year.

As well as the Sun, I have included the dates/times for the Full Moons (white circles with names) and the New Moons (shaded circles). The Full Moons happen when the Earth is inbetween the Sun and the Moon and the New Moons happen when the Moon is in between the Sun and Earth. There are slightly more than fourteen days between each of these 'Lunar Events'. I've used a bit of artistic licence with the naming of the Full Moons although my starting point was the translated names of the months on the Coligny Calendar.

The inner circle represents the Sun. Then there are the four Cross Quarter days/festivals (these are usually fixed at a specific day, or days of the year, so for example, Imbolc might be celebrated on 1st or 2nd February and people generally won't really need an exact time unless they want to use a specific event such as when the Earth/Sun is at 315 degrees - which can be worked out to the nearest second if needs be).

The Equinoxes and Solstices are shown next and these are generally aligned to the specific angles (0, 90, 180 and 270 degrees) and thus a specific time/date; and these are all rotated 180 degrees (half a year) for the Southern Hemisphere.

For the Zodiac Signs, I have included the degrees that align with the 'Tree Days' that they both share. So, for example, the start of the Days of Hawthorn is 9 degrees after the start of Aries.

As well as the Tree names, I have included the Irish/Celtic names and the Ogham lettering.

All of the times are for UK Local time (so take that into account when the clocks go forward and back). They would need to be adjusted for different time zones.

It was a fun challenge to understand everything that goes on to calculate the ephemeris/timings and to work out a way to present it that is as clear as possible - I used NASA's data via their 'Horizons' Web Interface.

BRIGID BRIGHT

Brigid Bright, Embrace the Light
Within, without, Erase all Doubt.
For Spring is near, The season turns,
Revealing Winter's inner burn.
Though Earth was sleeping, quiet, serene,
And Winter white hid all that's green,
Her Spirit moved the thoughts of all
In wait for Springtime's urgent call.
For time is moving ever faster,
Discoveries Great to sad Disasters,
And we must hold to all that's True,
The Oldest Old, the Newest New.
The Heat of Brigid's Triple Fires,
Burn brightly in a Holy pyre,
We honor Brigid's Triple Flames,
Recite in gratitude Her Names,
For smithcraft's meeting body's needs,
For shelter, transport, daily ease,
For beauty in both home and dress,
For in our work, our mind's progress.
For healing arts of herb and hand,
For quickening of the fallow land,
For multiplying flocks and herds,
For tempering counselors' soothing words.

For inspiration in all Art,
We pray for more of Brigid's Heart,
And let us bless the World this spring,
With all these gifts, Our Lady brings.

by Sherree Lynn Bailey

~ MARC RHODES-TAYLOR ~
Artist and Writer

Luis the Rowan Tree
by Marc Rhodes-Taylor ©

Marc follows the Druid path and he is affiliated with OBOD, the BDO, The Pagan Federation, The Druid Network and The Irish Pagan School. He is currently working on a number of projects for a variety of publications including *Wyrd Times*, *Mythprint*, and *Cunning Folk*. He has also made several appearances in *Touchstone*, the OBOD newsletter, and also *Pagan Dawn*, the journal of the Pagan Federation. For this journal he has contributed an essay entitled, *Filidecht - Poetry and Divination*.

Thor and the Rowan Tree
by Marc Rhodes-Taylor ©

FILIDECHT ~ POETRY AND DIVINATION

The word *filidecht* refers to poetry, prophecy and extemporaneous song; from the word *fili* meaning poet or seer. The word *file* originally meant a person who can see, a seer, and it is still used in Modern Irish as the word for poet. A *filidh* was an order of learned poets who were able to coexist peacefully with the ecclesiastical authorities who came along, by diversifying into new roles including poets, seers, teachers, advisers to kings and queens, and witnesses of contracts. The *filidh* curriculum lasted for at least seven years, including memorising poetry, teaching, and being students. This might last from twelve to twenty years. In the Irish tradition of *filidecht* the student is hidden in darkness. In the ritual of the *tarb feis* they would wrap themselves in a fresh bull's hide, covering their eyes in order to seek inner vision. With the introduction of Christianity the *fili* took over from the Druids when that class was suppressed. The *fili* had the power to bless and curse and to divine, they also served the roles of genealogist, historian, magician, lawgiver, judge, counsellor and poet, while presiding over the making of kings. One king went mad on account of the satires made upon him by a satirical bard. The *Aes Dana*, or people of skill or craft, identifies the practitioners of certain professions in medieval Ireland; in contrast to the *aes trebtha* or farming community. The *Aes Dana* covered artisanship, speech and knowledge; including doctors, lawyers, judges, harpists, and blacksmiths. The *Aes Dana* enjoyed special status, with the law stipulating penalties for offenses against them and greater weight given on their evidence.

Filidecht was extremely important to the *Aes Dana*. The *fili* enjoyed the status of *nemed* putting them on a par with the king and the bishop. To them was entrusted the preservation and transmission of *senchas* which included the genealogies of the ruling family; the *dindshenchas*, or the lore of places and the origin legends of the tribe. They were credited with the power of prophecy; the *imbas forosnai* means encompassing knowledge which illuminates. The training of the *fili* required many years of education involving seven grades and three sub-grades. The role was hereditary, a *fili* had to be the son and grandson of a *fili*. Once he acquired this position, they were expected to behave as a *nemed*, to eulogise the king and to satirise injustices and to recite traditional tales for the king. Compared to this the bard was regarded as inferior; the bard being lacking in professional training. A bard was someone possessing natural ability who had not studied within the poetic schools. The *ollamh fodhla* or king of Ireland in druidic times built and endowed a college at Tara which was called the *mur ollamh* or the wall of the learned. All arts and sciences were represented there by the *ollaves* of music, history, poetry and oratory. The *ollaves* formed the great bardic association ruled over by the *ard file* or chief poet of Ireland. Music was taught by the *ollamhs* while the *brehons* intoned the laws and the *sennachies* chanted the genealogies of the kings. The poets recited the deeds of heroes and sang to their harps.

The chief bard was required to know four-hundred poems by heart; and the minor bard two-hundred. They were bound to recite any poem called for by the king. Once, the king demanded a recitation of the *tain bo cuailgne* but no-one knew it. *Seanchan* and the bards traversed Ireland under *geasa* or oath not to sleep in the same place until they had found the tale. Eventually it was revealed to them that only Fergus Roy knew the poem but he was dead, so they processed to his grave and stayed there for three days until Fergus stood up out of the grave and recited it. Finally the *brehons* enacted some strict regulations around the seventh-century under the command of King Aed, who tried to eradicate the *ollamhs*, poets and poetesses; but failed. He did reduce their privileges, revenues and numbers. The bardic association survived but lessened in power. The Brehon Laws decreed that a poet's horsewhip was to be taken from them until they had agreed to render justice; the horsewhip may actually have been a wand or staff of wood carrying verses written in ogham. By the thirteenth century the function of the *filidecht* was moved to the Bardic Schools.

* * *

Marc has a page on Flickr where you can see more examples of his artwork,

https://www.flickr.com/photos/183773182@N07/

Brigid of Brittany
by Marc Rhodes-Taylor ©

Brigid Triple Goddess
by Marc Rhode-Taylor ©

BRIGHID'S DANCE

When the rowan tree starts to unfurl
And the blackbird discovers a lost song
And the earth exhales winters last icy breath
She comes
When the rigid hawthorn starts to bow
And the insects chatter in clicks and whirs
And the forest floor shakes away the bones of fallen leaves
She wakes
In light and hope
With poetry
And the flaming forge
She comes
With healing hands
And silver springs
Through tiny seeds
She wakes
And now the skies are pierced with gold
And jewels of green adorn the hedge
Her pulse the beat that drives the chant
That brings the still to dance.

by Alison Pope

~ LORRAINE GOODISON ~
Artist and Writer

Saint Brigid
by Lorraine Goodison ©

Lorraine writes ~ I think of myself as a shamanic medium. My spiritual path began with shamanic traditions and evolved into mediumship, drum/vibrational work, spiritual art and lately, vocal energy healing...

Birth of the Phoenix
by Lorraine Goodison ©

Lorraine continues ~ I write poetry and prose, sing to trees, am passionate about standing stones and Neolithic symbolism; and I am a servant to a cat. I am also a member of a tribal/Celtic fusion dance group called Treubh Dannsa.

www.facebook.com/treubhdannsa

Sacred Oak Labyrinth by Lorraine Goodison ©

Mysteria by Lorraine Goodison ©

WHEN BRIGID ENTERED MY LIFE

During what I think of as my 'pagan years', I wasn't drawn to the deities like some. I had a vague reverence for The Goddess which sat beside my equal vagueness toward The God. I sat on the edge of the circle, unsure where my place might be. Then one Imbolc, Brigid introduced Herself.

I was invited to a friend's house in Fife, to join them in celebrating Imbolc. We were a small group; four women and two men. I had no real idea what was being done as our host, Catherine, organised the blessing of the hearth while the men took themselves outside to tend the bonfire and to sing. The house was the domain of the women, this night.

There was a throne already created in the conservatory with photographs of ancestors, ivy, snowdrops, and rowan, decorating the space. The other women, familiar with this ritual, debated who would take on the mantle of Brigid. Jane volunteered. We were each given snowdrops to weave into her hair before she wrapped a hooded cloak around her and left to wander the dark garden on her own. I understood that she was going to connect to the energy of Brigid but I didn't have a clue what that really meant. I was as green as a new bud.

In a low voice, Catherine told me that when Brigid came in, we were not to look directly at her as that would be disrespectful. "Okay..." I thought.

The conservatory door opened and in came Jane. Only she wasn't Jane. She was – other. She was Goddess, contained and powerful. As she walked toward her throne, she looked directly at me. I saw and felt Brigid's presence through those human eyes and I knew Her.

The full details of that night have unravelled in my memory but I will never forget the impact of the Goddess Brigid's gaze. Since then, She has made Herself known to me in many ways.

by Lorraine Goodison ~ **www.lightwithin.weebly.com**

Come now child, with your bread and tea, pull up a chair and sit with me.

I'll tell you how there came to be the legend of the Rowan Tree...

For long ago, one fateful night,
a chalice lost brought forth a fight
of good and evil, of wrong and right,
carried out upon an Eagle's flight.
Drops of blood and severed feathers
from the battle drifted down
the two took root, through wind and weather,
buried deep within the ground.
What happened next brought forth the legend,
as seed turned into sprout,
born out of courage and fierce protection,
to keep all evil out.
The seedling grew with spirit,
'twas enchanted from the start
and those who gathered near it
did observe its sacred heart.
The further it developed
it became quite clear to see
to anyone who came around
this rare, transcendent tree.

Its foundation held the essence
and the power to make wise,
to bring courage and protection
like the Eagle when he flies,
to inspire those who seek it,
and to comfort those who cry,
to heal the sick, make strong the weak,
with each day's new sunrise.
Its twigs weaved into crosses
tied with bright red string, or yarn,
hang in dwellings for protection,
or held close, as lucky charms.
Its blood-red autumn berries
make fine wine or Christmas jam,
and symbolize the battle
that took place above the land.
And thus, my child, is how this
fabled story came to be...
'Tis magic in the legend
of the Earth's first Rowan Tree.

BLESS
INSPIRE
...
PROTECT

Poetry by Kelly Grettler / Artwork by Jenny Catalano

Legend of the Rowan Tree
by Jenny Catalano ©

THE LEGEND OF THE ROWAN TREE

Come now child, with your bread and tea,
Pull up your chair and sit with me.
I'll tell you how there came to be
The legend of the Rowan Tree.

* * *

For long ago, one fateful night,
A chalice lost brought forth a fight
Of good and evil, of wrong and right,
Carried out upon an Eagle 's flight.

Drops of blood and severed feathers
From the battle drifted down
The two took root, through wind and weather,
Buried deep within the ground.

What happened next brought forth the legend,
As seed turned into sprout,
Born out of courage and fierce protection,
To keep all evil out.

The seedling grew with spirit,
'Twas enchanted from the start
And those who gathered near it
Did observe its sacred heart.

The further it developed
It became quite clear to see
To anyone who came around
This rare, transcendent tree.

Its foundation held the essence
And the power to make wise,
To bring courage and protection
Like the Eagle whcn he flies,

To inspire those who seek it,
And to comfort those who cry,
To heal the sick, make strong the weak,
With each day's new sunrise.

Its twigs weaved into crosses
Tied with bright red string, or yarn,
Hang in dwellings for protection,
Or held close, as lucky charms.

Its blood-red autumn berries
Make fine wine or Christmas jam,
And symbolize the battle
That took place above the land.

And thus, my child, is how this
Fabled story came to be...
'Tis magic in the legend
Of the Earth's first Rowan Tree

**www.celticnationsmagazine.com/celtic-reviewer-
blogs/catalano-connection/**

www.kellygrettler.com

~ NELL ~
Artist

Phantom Queen
by Nell ©

Nell writes ~ I live in the republic of Ireland and I practice a Druidish style of paganism. My call is to the arts. My return to drawing has been part of my journey and recovery from some of life's traumas. All of my work, in regards to the divine, aspires to portray divinity with dignity.

Mother Goddess
by Nell ©

Nell continues ~ As a survivor of sexual exploitation I found some of the modern arts, dedicated to divinity, bordering on pornography. It's not a style I appreciate personally, so I felt moved to offer gentler more dignified art works. This may not be agreeable with everyone but this is my journey and my aspiration, Divinity with Dignity.

Prophecy
by Nell ©

Nell manages a small, private, Facebook group called Divine Inspiration; and whilst it is a private group Nell invites others to join, to share and contribute.

www.facebook.com/groups/1546186172437590

~ THALIA BROWN ~
Artist and Poet

Brigid of Glastonbury, banner
by Thalia Brown ©

Thalia's description of the *Brigid of Glastonbury* banner

Brighid ablaze with inspiration, stands on the peat earth of the Sea Moors. Invoking her perpetual flame, the hearth fire. She stands in a gateway of trees, with Rowan to the right and Silver Birch to the left. A pair of swans are her guardians, the winged and immortal presence of the Tuatha Dé Danann. The wolf is her companion, inspired by the stained glass in St John's church. A reminder of that spark of ancient inspiration to befriend the wild wolf and establish guard dogs that protect the flocks.

Her colours are white, red, and green; colours of Rowan the faery tree. Brighid's green mantle weaves its way around the earth, to bring beauty, regeneration, and renewal. Her two serpents are waiting to emerge when the year warms towards Spring. Twelve of Brighid's titles are painted in the border; above and below the flames of the four blacksmith's cauldrons, and on the four hourglasses of sun and moon.

The inspiration for this painting is twelve titles of Brighid. I painted it in 1994, when I was pregnant, as a blessing for my hearth and home. I was living close to St John's church, on its medieval burial ground. I painted the Cretan labyrinth in the earth beneath her feet, to symbolise the spiral journey that brings us home to our deepest essence.

In 2007 a strange synchronicity happened when the Glastonbury Tercentennial Labyrinth was created in the grounds of St John's Church. In 2015 I became Guardian of this Labyrinth - it seems the Goddess works in mysterious ways, or maybe creativity immerses us in that space where all time is now.

The twelve Brigid titles are:

Brea Saighit, Fiery Arrow
Bride Radiant Flame of Gold
Brighde of the Peat Heap
Brighde friend of Women Folk
Brighde of the White Swans
Brighde Conception of the Wave
Brighid of Prophecy
Bride of the Shores
Brigit of the Mantle
Brigit of the Kine
Woman of Healing
Bride of Joy

The banner, which is four foot square, now belongs to the Glastonbury Assembly Rooms and is often used at the Imbolc community celebrations.

* * *

Thalia is a visionary artist, and she designs and paints drapes, mandalas, and altar cloths; as tools for walking in beauty and awakening consciousness. In 2012 she became a bard, and druid, of The Druid Clan of Dana; and she seeded her own Grove – The White Hart of Avalon. Thalia works within the sacred landscape of the Glastonbury Zodiac, with the energies of the land, and she is also a yoga teacher.

Facebook ~ **The Grove of the White Hart of Avalon**
Facebook ~ **Gentle Yoga with Thalia**

Thalia continues ~ the poem and photograph below were inspired by a bee gathering pollen from a flowering Rowan Tree at the Dove arts centre; in Libra of the Glastonbury Zodiac. The Rowan tree is in an Ogham tree circle, which was planted thirty years ago, its creation was inspired by the book *The White Goddess*, by Robert Graves.

ROWAN OF INSPIRATION

Rowan cup of inspiration
Bright is the burning tree,
Luis, the Fiery Arrow.
Follow the hum of the bee,
Dive deep, into Rowan,
Ablaze with flowers.

Embrace quiet ecstasy,
Drinking the nectar of divinity
Cool and intoxicating
These darts of faery fire
Ignite, the sinews of my mind,
With awen song of inspiration
Flow of spirit awakened.

by Thalia Brown

~ ANTHONY GAMMON ~
Prose

SPIRIT OF BRIGHID, GODDESS OF FIRE

As Druidic folk we look not only at the physical aspects of our world but the deeper spiritual aspects of the natural world around us; in both it's light and dark aspects.

The flame of a candle alone proves this as the flame dances it can create a shadow of our darker aspect dancing also, showing us the polarity of light and dark, reminding us that as humans we possess these traits within.

This mode of thinking takes me to Brighid who makes her presence felt from the time of Imbolc; and throughout the lighter days of the spring and summer months.

Although Brighid is often associated with healing waters such as wells, she is also a fire Goddess; thus linking us with the sun.

Most of us often forget our flame within connecting us with our spirit and the ether which helps us radiate as beings of light, our true aspect that most of us use as a focus point during meditation.

I often feel that the spirit of Brighid encourages us to look deep within the flame of our hearts to help us not only to connect with the source but to encourage us to do the same and also enjoy the warm beauty of life itself which can sometimes be dark.

As Brighid leaves her footprints on the Earth spreading love and happiness, this not only reminds us of our fire within, but to remain grounded too.

* * *

~ TRICIA HUTCHINSON ~
Artist

The Great Bear by Tricia Hutchinson ©

Tricia writes ~ The Great Bear is a spirit animal who has been guiding me at the moment on a very personal journey. She represents the culmination of a very challenging dark night of the soul I have experienced for a number of years... I had no idea really that the Bear was symbolic of Brighid and to older bear cults, but it explained what the movie *Brave* was getting at haha.

Instagram ~ **@nature_of_spirit**

~ ROSEMARY HANSON ~
Artist and Poet

THE SWAN

The Swans song is here
Just where you knew it would be my dear.
Held within your heart in soft embrace.
Now let the river flow your love to me.
For this your song is perfect grace.
for this your song is perfect grace.

Rosemary writes ~ I love Swans. My Limelight Essence of Swan led me to draw a vision I had of a Swan with a Cygnet on her back. I was sitting on a Tumuli looking towards Stonehenge and later I found the Swan in a little Wiltshire village on the river Tess.

~ FRANKLIN LAVOIE ~
Artist and Poet

Close up detail of *Brighid, Triple Goddess of Erin*
by Franklin LaVoie ©

Franklin has been an enthusiastic encourager of the Ogham Grove, Facebook group. He has a lovely intricate way of cramming many little details into his paintings; and a wonderful way of painting with words. Here are some of his inspiring pieces of awen.

I feel the deep ancestral resonance of joyous song, feeling it run through my bones; it excites the air, filling the space with a golden haze, invisible tones of coherent energy. Filling with nwyfre, from a thousand streams that converge in pulses, from artisan wellsprings of awen, gargling through the underground streams, bubbling with inspiration from the Holy Wells...

Brighid, Triple Goddess of Erin
by Franklin LaVoie ©

and the Hollow Hills - the henge stones. Like a bow that excites the string, and fills the body with sound, so the whole island of Albion, fills its lungs with the hum and whirrr of birdsong, carrying fresh notes above and below. Whales sing in the shimmering depths. Green waves like the rolling drums of Gwydion rock the forest canopy. The heavens mark the Time along with the tides. Slowly swelling chorus rises from the molten core, entraining the whole of Creation, and from the point (a pregnant pause) the Perpetual Choirs fill the air with beautiful melodies unheard since the world was young. Nature vibrates like a lover in a swoon. The eagle and the dove descend and bless this wholesome intention.

The Old Growth Forest - I spent hours hiking in the Old Growth Forest at the Deerlick yesterday. Ancient trees of many species stand 120 feet tall if they're a foot, and baring the marks, the scars, and deformities of surviving the centuries, through their astonishing performances of stoic temperance and titanic might. Their fluttering leaves whispering to reveal the invisible breath of the winds, scintillating the canopy of myriad greens in marblesque patterns, ebbing like the sea. Now and again, some living sentry of the haunting paradise gives voice in weird strains, or a momentary percussive rattle, in utterance of its incomprehensible effort to stand tall, hold fast the earth and stones, and stretch its limbs to capture the blazing sun like a whale opening its maw to feed on krill. Winding passages all up and down the miles of trails, wild old tenements of lichen; and fresh colonies of mushrooms that greet the senses with unbridled curiosity, naked as jaybirds, bashful as children, living proof that the dead rise with fresh eyes and gaze upon a world strangely familiar and completely new.

Maiden, Mother, Crone by Franklin LaVoie ©

RITES OF ROWAN

Shining eyes in candlelight heralding a blessed rite
Shadows lean across the night embracing each neophyte
Like bears climbing the mountain's height
for crystal caves, to reunite, thus
Earth and heaven turn the tides, as
lover's lissome limbs entwined
Their sacred berth the years beguile
Brigantia's stile, the delight of the eye
Twilight fades to tourmaline silhouetting trees between
the worlds. Witchbane perched on a dragon spine
Where snowdrops drink hallowed moonshine
Berries bright as the scarlet skies,
Swayed when the crimson mallard flies,
Fall with the pitter-patter of rain
Until their rapture fades, like mists swirl,
Baring branches hewn for the mundane world.

by Franklin LaVoie

Franklin LaVoie lives in Buffalo, New York, America, He
is a musician and a puppeteer storyteller. You can visit his
Facebook page, The Puppet Wagon, to find out more.

www.facebook.com/puppetwagon

I have awarded Helena the above Mistletoe 'Elen' charm, for my favourite poem – *She Walks By Sunlight* - which I have placed in the front of this journal on page 3.

GWYDION ~ BORN OF TREES

I am a leaf of an ancient tree,
The blackthorn's crown
And the hawthorn's wreath.
I am the one who was born of trees,
I am the one who knows them all.

The oak of might, and the gorse of gold,
The memory of alder, its roots and leaves,
The ivy and vine, with all its fruit,
I am the one who was born of trees,
I am the one who knows them all.

Springtime fragrance of apple bark -
Fern and beechwood, and royal ash
Holly proud and evergreen -
I am the one who was born of trees,
I am the one who knows them all.

Fragrance of apples – as springtime fine,
Silvery tremble of poplar fair,
Birch of beginning, and yew of death -
I am the one who was born of trees,
I am the one who knows them all.

Rowan that burns among the snow,
Hazel of waters and forest glade
Elder of endings, and silent fir -
I am the one who was born of trees,
I am the one who knows them all.

Heather of hillsides and cliffs of grey,
Spindle of fate and the noble reed,
Honey that drips from the boughs high -
I am the one who was born of trees
I am the one who knows them all.

Groves and forests, the hills of green,
Wind that carries the news on high,
Swift, young rivers and olden seas
Gwydion knows what lies in store,
Gwydion sees, and he knows it all.

by Helena Sobolevskaya

There is a lot of stuff posted on Facebook, passing by, most of it is inane and of little significance. But there are gem-stones in the rubble too; diamonds in the dust. The poetry of Helena Sobolevskaya is one of those rare stones shining in a sea of mundane postings. Much of Helena's poetry hits a Celtic nerve; there is something 'old soul' in a lot of her writings. Something akin to the haunting nuance of Fiona Macleod that prickles the hairs upon one's neck.

WHAT FOREST KNEW

What aspen knew was how to come alive at the very first wave of his wand.

What ash knew, was how to sparkle and breathe magic at the very first word of his lips.

What oak knew was how to hide and heal the pain at the very first englyn of his song.

What willow knew was how to nourish and restore the heart at the very first sigh of his chest.

What heather knew was how to charm and create dreams at the very first gleam of his smile.

What rowan knew was how to protect and nurse the fae at the very first call of his voice.

What gorse knew was how to inspire and nurture the beauty with the very first wish of his eye.

What elder knew was how to ward off and repel at the very first motion of his hand.

What the birch knew was how to begin anew and lead at the very first glance of his eyes.

What the alder knew was how to defend and clear the ways at the very first request of his magic.

What the hawthorn knew was how to challenge and dare at the very first order of his conscience.

What the holly knew was how to change and give at the very first chant of his desire

What the hazel knew was how to seek and grant knowledge at the very first motion of his staff.

What the apple knew was how to light up and see beyond the ways given at the very first gesture of his fingers.

What the blackberry knew was how to gather in and harvest the dearest at the very first spell of his wisdom.

What the ivy knew was how to support and strengthen at the very first thought of his brightness.

What the fern knew was how to preserve and honor the truth at the very first enchantment of his making.

What the blackthorn knew, was how to enchant and beguile at the very first notion of his mind.

What the pine knew was how to observe and review at the very first spread of his staves.

What the poplar knew was how to animate and pulse with life at the very first quickening of his pulse

What the yew knew was how to persevere and transcend at the very first glimpse of his transformation.

What the spindle knew was how to weave and follow the destiny at the very first nod of his head.

What the honeysuckle knew was how to initiate and illuminate the experiences of spirit at the very first syllable of his mouth.

What the gooseberry knew was how to open and keep safe the ways of the ancestors at the very first touch of his hands

What the beech knew was how to move and confront the fears at the very first order of his voice.

What the trees knew was how to serve, obey and love him – for he was their life, their strength and their warden.

What the trees knew was his name, for this was the only thing they knew.

Gwydion.

by Helena Sobolevskaya

Helena describes herself as ~ born sometime in the twentieth century; somewhere between mountains and sky. Prefers to be known as a channeler, although writer and bard are also fine. Writing for more than ten years, she divides her time between two kids, writing, exploring Celtic myths and Otherworld journeying, tarot, design and crafting. She can be found on Facebook and wordpress,

www.facebook.com/groups/561613791435693

https://aneurinstree.home.blog/

~ CLAIRE GERRARD ~
Artist

Our Lady of the Bees
by Claire Gerrard ©

Claire writes ~ this was painted in 2019, shortly after Notre Dame Cathedral was damaged by fire. Bride's eyes well with tears where she stands among the pink roses and the yellow roses, nursing her bees back to health. Resurrection on her shining brow. Our Mother Bride is bigger than any church structure that tries to contain her. She is free of the old confines. Although wildfire raged through its ancient rafters, and her massive roof collapsed in avalanche, Bride's bees were spared, her golden emissaries were like grace under fire.

www.alchemicalartmaking.com

Beautiful photography of autumnal Rowan leaves by
Nia Walling. Please visit her Instagram account **@nia_walling**

* * *

A LITTLE CHANT FOR BRIGID

A candle for Brigid, my companion, my protector.
A candle for the healer, for the poet and the maker.
A candle for the Dagda, who's daughter you are.
A candle for your legend, flame of Kildare.
A candle for your glory, for fire, for water.
A candle for the goddess of the waters of Spring.

by Gary Washington

Gary Washington is a composer and OBOD druid. He lives in
the USA in the State of Maine. He can usually be found on
Facebook, when he isn't lost in the woods somewhere.

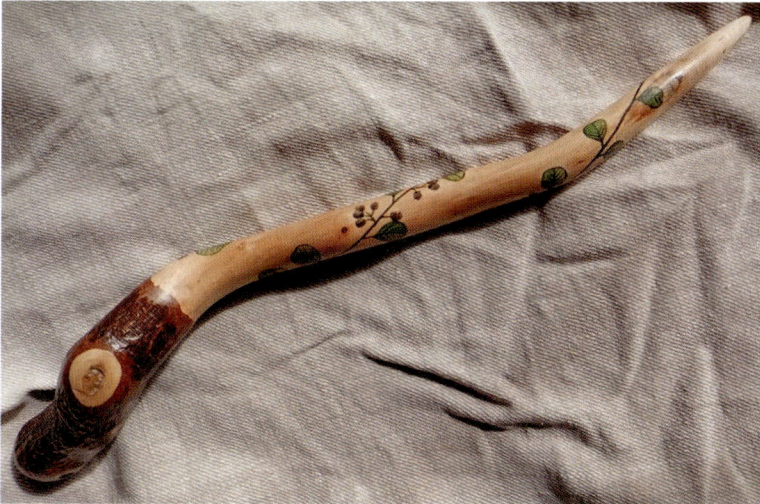

I have awarded Thea, the hand-painted Alder wand
(The Second Herald of Imbolc), for my favourite essay.

* * *

THE GREEN MANTLE OF BRIGID

I first became aware of Brigid in the form of St Brigid because my Gran, who was an Irish traveller, used to regularly pray to her. My Gran was beholden to no-one, fearless, but at the same time, stoic and stubborn. I remember her clinging to the small silvery St Brigid medal, part of her Rosary, when the rain hammered on the wooden roof and all the buckets inside were full, asking for relief or shelter. She made Brigid crosses from hay and dried grass, when she sat on her stool in the balmy summer evenings, a roll-up (cigarette) in her mouth, a huge tea pot at her side, blessing each one with unknown exotic (to me) words, before continuing to the next and the next. Brigid gave her comfort and guidance - she would swear this, even when her rheumatism made her unable to walk or use her hands. Her faith was absolute.

These memories of my Gran are cherished and remain absolutely clear, even though she passed away over thirty-five years ago. But saints and what I believed they represented, were something I felt little personal connection with. However as I spent time in my childhood living in the wilds and wild places, I have always experienced a strong sense of belonging to the forests and moors. I remember subliminally being aware of the spirit of woods and rivers as a child. I could sense the surging life-force of spring and the silent heartbeat of winter. The bond this formed was profound and inherent and I believe to this day, that we are one.

When my daughter was six or seven, I started following the Druidic path that had always been my destiny to do. One day, shortly after beginning Druidic training, I attended a workshop on Celtic Goddesses. Although it was a brief overview, my intention was to use it as a starting point, if you will, to future study and contemplation. It was here, I had an epiphany as I journeyed with Brigid in meditation. I suddenly knew that she had always been with me and was a protector of my daughter. I was immensely comforted, as though wrapped in swaddling cloths like a baby. Her healing love radiated through me like sunshine on new green leaves as they awaken. I wanted to shout from the highest mountain, I felt like Gwion Bach when he first tasted the three drops from the Cauldron of Inspiration and became Taliesin – I was completely alive for the first time.

From then on, the Goddess has been with me as my constant companion. I see and feel Her presence in every aspect of my life – from my daughter's infectious laughter, to each blade of grass under foot. I see Her in the glorious summer swelling of courgettes and apples in autumn, and the gentle blossom filled breezes of spring. I rest with Her in the snow covered death of winter, waiting to be re-born again every year.

Our favourite ritual is Imbolc, and we begin preparations during the previous autumn by planting twenty snowdrops each year, (nineteen for each flame-keeper and one for the Goddess who attends the sacred flame on the 20th day). As the ritual approaches we make Brideogs from the cut branches of our apple tree and cloth, in shades of green, to please the Goddess. On the eve of Imbolc we place the Brideog in her bed by the fireplace, and chant songs of devotion and praise.

Brideogs

A piece of cloth is hung outside in the hope that the Goddess will bless it as she walks by, and the mantle is used in healing and comport for the following year. I consult Her most nights through prayer, and give thanks for the blessings She has bestowed during each day. Her council is wise and honest and I often look at situations or issues anew – with fresh eyes, after meditating or asking for guidance.

Last year, I was working particularly deeply with my ancestors - my beloved Gran was constantly with me, guiding me to visit places in search of precious connections. My search lead me to Ireland, known as Her green mantle, where Brigid whispers in the rural greenness; and the kindness of strangers had Brigid's name imprinted throughout the land. I was guided to Kildare the birthplace of St Brigid, where there is a wonderful merging of pagan and Christian beliefs.

I was permitted to light two candles from the perpetual flame, kept by the welcoming nuns at Solas Bhride - one for my Gran to carry back to my family, and one to enable me to work more deeply with the fire aspect of the Goddess. I sat with two of the generous and open-hearted nuns and had a much appreciated discussion over steaming hot tea, about the Goddess, the saint, and my old Gran. Before I left, I underwent an overwhelming desire to present the Centre with my Gran's tiny nickel St Brigid medal. I hesitated because it is one of the only treasured commemorations I have of Gran. However, I instinctively knew that both Gran and the Goddess wanted me to do this.

Looking back at this visit, I now understand how the deep intrinsic love of Brigid has always been part of my ancestral DNA - through my Gran, and probably generations of her mother's before, continuing through myself and to my daughter. Now there is part of me in Kildare, connected to my ancestral mother-line through my Gran, and Beloved Brigid, saint and Goddess, as it has always been and will be, forever.

Thea Prothero is a professional photographer (amongst other things), and her work has appeared in *Pagan Dawn*; and she has her own website.

www.theaprothero.co.uk

~ COLLEEN KOZIARA ~
Artist

Brighid
by Colleen Koziara ©

Colleen is a prolific artist, she writes ~ My work is most often based upon a subject in nature, a myth or a legend. My images highlight the patterns in these subjects, not only of colour and form, but of energy and hidden meanings. My images are doorways. Where they take you, is up to you.

Manifesting Magical Mysteries
by Colleen Koziara ©

   Colleen's work can be viewed on a number of websites, please take a look at the following,

www.mysticalwillow.com

www.facebook.com/mystical.willow
www.fineartamerica.com/artists/colleen+koziara
www.etsy.com/shop/mysticalwillowart

Everything
by Colleen Koziara ©

Colleen continues ~ I currently specialize in two areas; artistic works which are considered Visionary Images and have about them a sense of being only partially grounded in this world, and working/teaching the arts with our Elders, aged 65 and older.

I would love to create magical Children's Books. Though I have not found it yet, somewhere there is a point, where these three pathways - Elders, Visionary Art, and Children's Books - meet and merge. That is the destination towards which I journey.

THE I AM OF BRIGHID

I am the fair maid and the gentle melt of snow
I am the spring bride and the black rod's cessation
I am the swan queen and the swift river flow
I am the new green shoot and the cow's sweet libation

I am the shining one and midwife of soul
I am the liminal shore, oystercatcher's sun
I am the pilgrim's lantern and way shown
I am the hearts yearning and ninth wave invitation

I am the flame, the blaze and the ember glow
I am the white wand and the fired imagination
I am the cunning that the serpent tongues know
I am the bard's muse and the wind's incantation

I am the forge and the mighty hammer blow
I am the healing balm and fiery purification
I am the warming light that seeks out each shadow
I am the truthful quill and its communication

I am the cosmic crown and the greening below
I am the call of the land beneath a nation
I am the hearth fire well-come to all as friend not foe
I am the kith and kin, the return and salvation

by Heidi Wyldewood

Heidi is a Spiritual Teacher, Mentor, Priestess, and Healer. She is particularly affiliated with Brighid and she wrote the above poem as an invocation intrinsic to a nationwide (UK) ritual that she orchestrated for Imbolc 2020; entitled 'Lift Up Her Light'. The intention of the ritual was to help heal the ancestral soul-trauma of the British

Isles - that had been caused by the conquest of the Roman Empire; in her own words,

'The intention for this was to help the national psyche of Britain re-member, to put back together, in a form of soul retrieval, itself. This re-membering will restore the connections to the spiritual roots, to its ancient Divine Mother, severed by the Roman Conquest woundings. This uprooting from the sacred in this way caused so much damage spiritually, that the eventual rampage and revenge of a wounded nation had long term devastating global impact. It is time to "sound the soul song".'

An Iron Age, Celtic, roundhouse.

The culture of the Brythonic Celts of Britain, and the Roman Empire, were as different as the left-brain and right-brain functionalities. The Britons lived in round houses, **circular** homes with hearth-fires in their very centres. They decorated their treasured items with designs of circles and spirals; and evidence suggests that they were primarily a matriarchal society – they had many gods and goddesses but the Great Mother was supreme, and Brighid/Brigantia (in a wide variety of different versions of her name) was honoured at every hearth-fire of every roundhouse. In stark contrast, the Roman Empire was very **square** – with square and rectangular buildings, and rectangular shields baring the thunder-bolts of Jupiter, King of the Gods.

The Henley Wood Mother Goddess, bronze figurine. Is a humble domestic altar-piece from a site in Somerset, UK. She wears a Celtic torc around her neck. Shown approximately life size.

'Boudica, the famous queen of the Iceni, waged war upon Rome at the same time that the Druids of Anglesey were being attacked; was her timing deliberate? Her actions distracted Suetonius Paulinus and he retreated from Anglesey and took his forces south to confront the Celtic queen. Did she seize the opportunity to attack the south-east whilst he was busy in the far west, or did she deliberately distract him from his bloody objective? We'll never know but her timing is a great intrigue. Boudica was defeated the following year, 61 AD, and she committed suicide rather than be humiliated by her enemies.'
(Yuri Leitch, *The Pagan Temple of Glastonbury Tor*)

Heidi's invocation, *The I Am of Brighid*, is intended to be used by others to help heal the trauma of the past. Heidi teaches a spiritual system called The Brighid Path; and you can find out much more about her on her website,

www.barefoot-heartsong.com

~ NIKKI SHABBO ~
Prose and Rowan Lore

THE ROWAN TREE
(Sorbus Aucuparia/Lady of the Mountains/Quicken Tree)

"I am the spirit of the Rowan tree,
All aspects of life will be found within me.

I am of the Rose Clan,
Built upon the five petals, or pentagram.

I have heart healing properties,
And act on the blood and circulation.
The five petals represent the five limbs* or the five elements.

I teach you to engage with your heart,
In right relationship with your limbs and actions
And thus your incarnation.
My five-petalled flowers are lunar and my berries** are solar.

I am able to grow and flourish in the most barren
And difficult of situations.
My life force is strong and determined.
My message is not to give up,
But to hold on strong to what you believe in
And to the power of your own life-force."

(Information given from a journey with my Rowan tree in October 2014)

*Both legs, both arms, and head.
** The Rowan berry also has a tiny five-pointed star opposite its
stalk. The pentagram, an ancient symbol of protection, is an
outward manifestation of the Rowan's protective powers, but
there is more to the magic than this.

(And from further work with my Rowan tree in November 2014):

"I am able to grow from the smallest of crevices
In the most inaccessible of spots.
My life-force energy is strong and determined,
Reflecting power, vitality, and tenacity.
My message is not to give up,
But to hold on strong to what you believe in
And to the power of your own life-force."

A photo taken near Whistman's Wood on Dartmoor,
in late summer 2014

So I intuit; being in the right relationship with yourself, and working with the Rowan, strengthens your personal power through strengthening your positive life-energy; which puts you in touch with your own power (higher self), thus giving you the potential of untangling anything (literally anything) which may have entrapped and weakened you. It is these aspects which makes the Rowan such a powerful ally. It it is not just the Rowan which protects you but you, yourself.

Rowan Correspondences

Planets: Sun and Mercury
Element: Fire
2nd consonant of the Ogham: Luis (pronounced LWEESH)
2nd tree of the Celtic tree calendar: approx 18th Jan to 5th Feb
Goddesses: Sequana, Brigid, Boann
Symbols: The three phases of the Goddess:
    White blossoms ~ Virgin/Maiden
   Red berries ~ Menstruating Woman/Mother
   Black bark ~ The Old, Wise Woman/Crone
Animal: Swan and Duck (both swans and ducks are of the Anatidae biological family and are linked with Brigid).

There is a Celtic song dedicated to the Rowan tree - 'Oh Rowan Tree' by John McDermott, which is easily found on the internet.

In botany the Rowan tree, Sorbus Aucuparia, is a member of the rose family, like the Hawthorn, the Apple, and the Blackberry.

In magic, the Rowan was said to be a help to witches, but could also drive them away.

The rowan tree in some mythology stands as the first tree in the world, from which all other plants are said to descend.

THE MYTH

In Finland, there is a myth that says the Rowan was the first tree. Rauni, is a Finnish name for the Rowan tree-goddess or spirit; and is also known in Sámi and Estonian mythology. She composes the sacred northern spiritual and mystical powers of the Rowan tree rituals. She is said to have descended from heaven when all the earth was bare and disguised herself as a Rowan tree. In her loneliness, she mated with the god of thunder, Ukko. Some sources say they were already partners. From the lightning bolt of mating resulted all the plants of the earth being birthed (this follows the concept of all life originating from fire/heat and water).

The word *raun* probably became rowan, and perhaps also *rune*. Rune staves were calendars, upon which were marked the days of the year, beginning with the first full moon after the winter solstice. They were carved in runes and notches onto rowan wood (this was a myth I was told whilst in the arctic circle in Finland over fifteen-years ago). Rauni is a great healer and knows how to eliminate pain in people; the berries are still being used today for stomach disorders.

In the Celtic tree ogham the Birch tree is the first tree and Rowan the second; however both trees are known to be among the first to colonise new ground so I guess it depends on local climates as to who is first.

What for me is of deeper interest is that the element associated with the Birch is water, and the Rowan is fire; so once again we have fire and water. The element of water is generally perceived today to be feminine or yin. Water in its natural state is horizontal. The element of fire is generally perceived today as masculine or yang. Fire in its natural state is vertical. These two energies at their highest vibration embody the fire of spirit and the waters of life; creating unconditional love that flows through our collective consciousness in the Noosphcre. Also more recently it has occurred to me that when fire and water come together we get steam or mist; the liminal state for Otherworld.

Rowan's other name's; Lady of the Mountain (for its love of growing in difficult places) and the name Quicken Tree, finds it's way back to the words quicken beam which means Tree of Life.

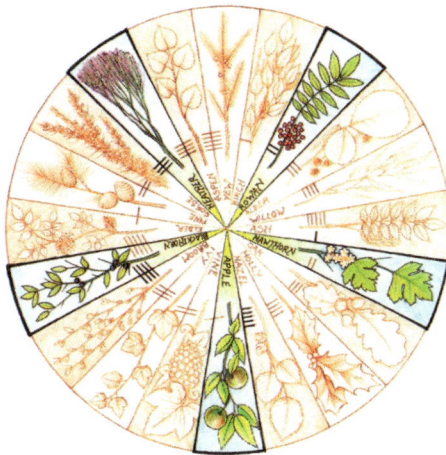

~ CORAH APLONIA AVALON ~
Essay

BRIDIE, BRIGHID, FFRAID, BLODEUWEDD
AND THE ROWAN TREE

Thig an nathair as an toll Lá donn Bríde
Ged robh trí troighean dhen t-sneachd Air leac an lair.

The serpent will come from the hole on the day of Bride
Though there should be three feet of snow
on the flat surface of the ground.

Bride, Bridie, the Shining Bright One with Her Red Flame

Bridie, Brighid, Brigit, Ffraid, Blodeuwedd, Triple Goddess with the many names, she is Maiden Bride and Crone Cailleach. It is said she was a daughter of the Tuatha Dé Danann, daughter of Dagda; a fairy folk descended from the stars. Later folklore tells that she was wife of Bres and had a son called Ruadán. She had two sisters, but this can be the association of the Triple Goddess. An Irish Goddess she was, of birth and re-birth; as she tends the Earth with Her Elemental Mantle through winter and spring into abundant times. She was the Bride who birthed the Earth through cycles and seasons, over and over again. She was the red flame who tended the heart of the Earth.

Sometimes she is called the Mother of the Tri Dée, as Daná or Danu, Dan/Don of the Tuatha Dé Danann, or Danube Tribe. The Children of Daná called her the Earth Mother. Her name has changed though, so many times, as stories do. She had magical powers, milking the cows and creating abundance and healing for all. She 'travelled' with the ever-changing seasons, at one with nature and the cosmos above; giving honey and milk, as we journey through the Milky Way in the Universal Void. A cosmic mystery and natural rhythm many have forgotten these days.

Today we mostly remember her as Saint Brighid, which is related from the 6th century. Her convent was in Kildare, her flame tended from the 17th century by nineteen nuns. In Glastonbury we find Bride's Well and Mound. She travelled with St Patrick and founded a convent on Beckery (Little Ireland), a most sacred place; in the 6th century. A chapel has been found in excavations and legend has it that this was the chapel of the Arthurian stories where Arthur saw a vision of the Virgin Mary – but it is was actually an old Brighid chapel.

Bridie, Bride, Bless the Earth with fertile new Birth

In primal Celtic times her name was Blodeuwedd, 'Flower Face', created through the elements from nine flowers/plants, for the god Lleu (Lugh). She was one of five goddesses of the Celtic pantheon of ancient Avalon. Here the ancient mysteries of earth are founded in geometrical and elemental symbols. She is mentioned in *The Mabinogion*. Her season was the birth and re-birth of the earthly time, Imbolc (Oimelc, Imbolg). New birth, new life, as all starts again upon Mother Earth in her ever changing Wheel of Life. As the Wheel of course rolls on its journey through the Universe, and Time, the seasons shift with the directions. Now through the last 26,000 years, we are again in Imbolc as we know Imbolc around the beginning of February. It has never been a vast calendar day as most celebrate these days, our calendar is the rhythm and flow of Earth in her cosmic dance with the Universe. This moment in time beholds the first birth, but also the seeding of all new, which unfolds around Lammas, through the cycling of interconnection with the seasons. Inner wisdom, Inner child, pure, discovering the earth anew, like a baby observing and searching for movement and finding wisdom to be. She is a maiden in the day and an owl in the night; bringing us back to the Maiden and the Crone, or Cailleach if you like. As God and Goddess come together during the fertile season of Beltaine, she is the Bride, the pure one, to grow into womanhood and to be prepared for the union.

So what were her names through Time: In old Irish it was Brigit and Brighid; and Brid in modern times. Early English names were Bridget, Bridgit. In French it became Brigitte. In Italy, Germany, and Holland, Brigida. In Finland it is Piritta and in Sweden Birgitta. The sound of the old Brigit has stayed quite the same here, only the primal Celtic goddess Blodeuwedd had a different sound. In much later times the name in England changed to Brittania; as in the Land. Briganti means 'the High One', named after the goddess Brigantia. While in old German, Germaans, the name became Burgunt, later Burgundy, where old lines exist. Land borders were quite different in those days, so Holland, Germany and France were in a slightly different alignment with their land borders. In Scotland they call her Brighde or Bride and in Wales her name can be Ffraid, Braid, Braint or Breint. In Anglesey a river is named after her, and in Wales some place names are; Llansanffraid, 'Saint Bride's Village', and Llansaniffraid-ym-Mechain. And so we are back to the name Brid or Bride, the White One, Shining One, the Bride.

Rowan Tree

The Rowan's name derives from the Scottish Gaelic word 'rudha-an', meaning the red one. It is considered to be a sacred tree in tree lore, and it is associated with the Celtic goddess Brighid; patroness of the arts, fire, smith work, sacred flame, healing, spinning, and re-birth. As Imbolc is a Cross Quarter Fire Festival and Bridie is associated as the 'Bright' and sometimes the 'Red Haired' with her 'Red Flame', you can imagine how this trinity - Imbolc, Bride, and Rowan - fit together perfectly through this seasonal celebration. In Scotland and Ireland, spinning wheels and spindles were traditionally made out of rowan wood; also dowsing and divining rods. A rowan wand, walking or talking stick, will guide and protect you.

Rowan is the tree of power, causing life and magic to flower.
New life, new birth,
Rowan is also called 'the Lady of the Mountains'.
January 18th – February 5th in the Ogham Tree Alphabet.
Its element is Fire – giving life.
Its colours: red, white and green.

Rowan protects house and hearth, it's magical protection has long been used to ward off enchantment and lightning. It's flame-red berries bear the sign of the pentagram, the five-pointed star, and it is said that a rowan whip or branch can break spells. The five-pointed star connects her with the cycle of Venus and the elemental mysteries on Earth. A cross made of rowan and bound with red thread was used by our ancient ancestors as a protective charm above the doors of houses - as sung and celebrated in the ancient rhyme:

Rowan tree, red thread,
Holds the evil and ills all in dread.'

So Brighid, Brigit, or any way you wanna write her name, also called the 'Bright One', the 'Shining One' with her 'Red Flame' and her Sacred Rowan Tree. The power of the Rowan tree gives birth, life, and attracts life-giving ideas/projects, as the Rowan's berries attract birds. Rowan is one of the first trees to bud, the seeds are stirring, patience is asked, all comes in its own time; promise is near. In later times it's wood, flowers, and berries were used in protection against evil, elements, elementals, and elves. Rowan is good for protection, very helpful with clearing the mind and opening up for new ideas, for re-birth and inspiration of heart. It opens perspective, connects nature and gives space for deep understanding of remembering your true essence here on Earth and your role in the universal flow.

For the Celts the Rowan tree was a symbol of all the hidden mysteries on earth, and in nature, and it holds the key to awakening and quickening the life force within. In Scottish tradition it was used a little differently, as folklore tells, Rowan wood was only used in ritual; and ritually made amulets.

Brighid and Rowan tree, how Magic unfolds as we let Nature in,
Goddess of the Flame, Healing, Poetry,
Smith Crafting and re-Birth,
Bride, Brighid, Blodeuewedd; it's the sound that gifts the symbol.

Bridie Maiden, Crone and Cailleach

In Gaelic, Irish and Scottish, Celtic traditions, the Cailleach is the ancestor deity as well as the Divine Hag; she is also 'Creatrix', a creation and weather deity, connected with all in Nature. She is known as the *Cailleach Bhéara(ch)* or *Bheur(ach)*; and these words literally mean 'old woman, hag'; she is also the wise one, the Crone. The name comes from the Old Gaelic *Caillech* meaning 'veiled one', another word is *caille*, 'mantle' or 'veil', so 'Veiled One' - Bridie's Mantle, Triple Goddess, Cailleach.

So let me, the Cailleach, tell you a little story...

My name is often referred to as the Cailleach Bhéara(ch), Cailleach Bheur(ach), or diverse variations of that. I am even associated with the Cow Goddess and the horned creatures; but also with Winter, darkness, wilderness, and the Wise Hag. I can be the one and the many, and I have many, many, names; such as Digde, Old Woman, and Milucra. In the tale of the Glas Gaibhnenn I am called Biróg, I am also called Brid, Buí or *Bua(ch)* or the *Caillagh*. There have been many names and meaning through Time, explaining, or trying to explain, my existence and sound.

Cailleach is *Cailleacha or Ki-laxe* in Irish, *Cailleachan* in Scottish Gaelic and *Caillaghyn*. The meaning of the word is found, for example, in Gaelic, *Cailleach-dhubh* (a nun) and *Cailleach-oidhche* (an owl); yes, as well as the Irish *Cailleach feasa* (wise woman, fortune-teller) and *Cailleach phiseogach* (sorceress, charm-worker) - to name a few. Then we have the Gaelic *Caileag* and the Irish *Cailín* (young woman, girl), and *Caile* (woman), and the Lowland Scots *Carline/Carlin* (old woman, witch). And they found out that the Irish *Síle*, (hag), is a connection between the Cailleach and the stone carvings of Sheela Na Gigs. So many stories, through so many times.

RUIS (Elder) by Yuri Leitch
(An illustration for book one of *The Chronicles of Ogus*)

In Scotland I am known as Beira, Queen of Winter; I am the Creatrix of numerous mountains and high hills, which have been formed when I was striding across the land and accidentally dropped rocks from my *creel* or wicker basket. Some say I build the mountains intentionally, to serve as my stepping stones. I carry a hammer for shaping the hills and valleys, and yes I am also the Mother of all of the goddesses and gods. I am the personification of Winter, the white world and stillness between the turning of the wheel. I am herding my deer, tending springs, and my staff freezes the ground - I'm the 'One with the Cauldron'.

Sometimes I am twinned with the goddess Brìghde, when the Cailleach is seen as a seasonal deity or spirit of the Wheel, ruling the winter months between Samhain and Beltaine. It's all interpretations to symbolise the essence, you know. Some interpretations have the Cailleach and Brìghde as two faces of the same goddess, while others describe the Cailleach as turning into stone at Beltaine and reverting to humanoid form at Samhain; in time to rule over the winter months. Here I am the Queen of Winter again. The change of power between the Winter Goddess and the Summer Goddess was celebrated in ancient times at any time between *Là Fhèill Brìghde* (Imbolc) and Beltaine. It is said that the first signs of spring may be named after either the Cailleach or Brìghde. They were wise the ancients, still in contact with us, in nature and in between the worlds.

There is a Scottish story about a stone at a sacred site, and at every turning of the year they celebrate ceremonially by resetting the stone for a new year cycle; for fertility and peace on the Land, it goes like this: There is a place called Glen Cailleach, which joins to Glen Lyon, in Perthshire. The glen has a stream named Alt nan Cailleach. This area is famous for an ancient ritual which according to legend is associated with the Cailleach. There is a small shieling (a shelter) in the glen, known as either Tigh nan Cailleach, or Tigh nam Bodach, which houses a series of apparently carved stones. According to local legend they represent the Cailleach, her husband the Bodach, and their children. This local legend suggests that the Cailleach and her family were given shelter in the glen by the locals and while they stayed there the glen was always fertile and prosperous. When they left they gave the stones to the locals with the promise that as long as the stones were put out to look over the glen at Beltaine and put back into the shelter and made secure for the winter at Samhain, then the glen would continue to be fertile. This ritual is still carried out to this day. The Cailleach is still honored through many ways.

Cailleach or Brìghde, she speaks...
Là Fhèill Brìghde (Imbolc) is also the day the Cailleach gathers her firewood for the rest of the winter. Legend has it that if she intends to make the winter last a good while longer, she will make sure the weather on Imbolc is bright and sunny, so she can gather plenty of firewood to keep herself warm in the coming months - as a result, people are generally relieved if *Là Fhèill Brìghde* is a day of foul weather, as it means the Cailleach is

asleep, will soon run out of firewood, and therefore winter is almost over.

On the Isle of Man, where I am known as *Caillagh ny Groamagh*, the Cailleach is said to have been seen on St. Bride's day in the form of a gigantic bird, carrying sticks in her beak. In Scotland, Cailleachan, old women, are also known as the Storm Hags, and seen as personifications of the elemental powers of nature; especially in a destructive aspect. They are said to be particularly active in raising the windstorms of spring, during the period known as *A' Chailleach*.

I am also related to the Corryvreckan whirpool (between the islands of Jura and Scarba). In Scottish Gaelic, *Coire Bhreacain* means 'Cauldron of the Plaid' or 'Washtub of the Cailleach' - quite a washtub don't you think? The process of washing the plaid/cloak takes three days; a ceremonial cleansing rite. After the washing, the plaid or cloak is again pure white, and snow covers the land – and did you hear of Bridies Mantle covering the land?

In Scotland and Ireland, the first farmer to finish the grain harvest made a corn dolly, representing the Cailleach, also called the 'Carlin' or 'Carline', from the last sheaf of the crop. The corn dolly would then be tossed into the field of a neighbor who had not yet finished bringing in their grain. The last farmer to finish had the responsibility to take in and care for the corn dolly for the next half a year, with the implication they'd have to feed and house the Hag all winter. After all, She is the Hag of Wisdom, Healing, and Counsel. Then with Imbolc the corn dolly was made into a Bridie Doll; and here is old tradition.
So the Cailleach has spoken...

There is so much to tell about the Maiden and the Cailleach, from Ireland to the Highlands, from Wales to the many isles. So many stories to tell; these are only a few I have shared. So that brings us back to Brighid, the Bride, who re-births through her flowering nature. Let Her energy guide you in creativity, let her flame bring passion into your hearts and heal, and may you re-birth with her in the flow of Life.
Bendithion Bridie, Brighid, Cailleach Bearra

www.traditionalavalonmysteryschool.com

Facebook ~ **Traditional Avalon Mystery School**

~ JENNIFER MOORE ~
Artist

MY WHEEL OF THE YEAR

Jennifer writes ~ I was very inspired after reading Yuri Leitch's book *The Ogham Grove: The Year Wheel of the Celtic/Druidic God Ogma the Sun-Faced*. I was really fascinated when I saw Yuri's artwork titled 'The Ogham Grove' where he combined the Ogham with the Zodiac and the twelve months into a wheel of the year. I have always been intrigued by symbolism and connections and patterns; and when I discovered Yuri's Ogham Grove it sparked Imbas inside me. I used Yuri's wheel of the year that he created, and created my own.

The four pentagrams (found in Yuri's book on page 63): I followed Yuri's lead with using the colour green to represent the Winter Solstice Pentagram of Yew, Holly, Ivy, and Pine. As Yuri explained (page 64) there's 'one odd tree out' which is the Willow. I chose the red colour which followed Yuri's concept of the Summer Solstice Pentagram of Apple, Blackthorne, Rowan, and Hawthorne; with Heather being the odd one out. For the Spring Equinox Pentagram I researched the pioneer trees and corresponded with Yuri's white pentacle of Birch, Hazel, Broom and Gorse, with Ash as the odd one out.

For the Autumn Equinox Pentagram I wanted to use an Autumn colour so I researched some similarities between the remaining five trees - plants which include Alder, Aspen, Oak, Vine, and Elder. I was able to find a connection that all five have some link to the colour orange. I found that Alder wood bleeds a dark orange colour when cut. The Aspen's leaves often turn orange in Autumn. As Oak wood ages it often turns orange; also the leaves of the Oak may change to orange in the Autumn. For the Vine I found that there are golden orange grapes to make orange wine. In America we have red Elderberry trees and their berries can change to an orange colour before ending in a bright red colour; also their leaves turn a beautiful orange in the Autumn.

For each month I chose the tree that resonates most with me, so I chose Birch for January, Rowan for February, Willow for March, Oak for April, Holly for May, Apple for June, Vine for July, Broom for August, Elderberry for September, Pine for October, Aspen for November, and Yew for December. For the Zodiac signs I painted each according to the four elements to which they correspond. The outer ring represents the eight fire festivals of the Celtic year that are observed along with a few symbolic items for each of events.

~ THE BRIGHID AND ROWAN ICON ~
by Yuri Leitch

Here is an explanation of the symbolism used in the Brighid Icon shown on page 1 of this journal.

In the foreground is the Romano-British bas-relief of Brigantia, from Birrens in northern Britain; which is probably the oldest known representation of Brighid in the British Isles (3rd to 4th century AD). Her symbolism is heavily influenced by the Roman goddess, Minerva – goddess of wisdom and protection – as well as all arts, including music, poetry, and medicine (which are divine characteristics shared by the Gaelic goddess Brigid). The primary symbols of Brigantia, her spear and shield, have been continued into the modern era as the attributes of the personification of the British Isles, Brittania. An old fifty-pence piece, adorned with Brittania, can thus serve as a great 'lucky charm' of Brighid/Brigantia.

At the base of Brigantia's spear is an omphalos (egg-stone) that marks the sacred centre, or navel, of her territory – which can be a tribal territory, the centre of a kingdom, the centre of one's self, and the centre of the northern hemisphere night sky. The central stars (those that never set) are the circumpolar constellations – Ursa Major (Great Bear), Ursa Minor (Little Bear), Draco (Dragon) and Cassiopeia (the Queen of Heaven) – all are depicted within this icon (the mother bear and cub; the red serpent energy for Draco, flowing up Brighid's spear; and the W-shape of Cassiopeia rests upon her breasts).

As well as being tools of protection, Brighid's spear and shield also represent the circumference/boundary of a sacred grove and the vertical axis that connects the centre-point of a territory to the centre of the heavens. Thus she offers both the tools of protection and the means by which one can connect, within, to the centre of all things – a bit like the story of Jack and the Beanstalk.

Bears and serpents (Draco) hibernate in the winter and then return again in the spring – this is akin to Brighid's annual festival of Imbolc, which marks the beginning of spring.

Brighid's shield is decorated with three swans and a triskelion (triple spiral) in honour of the Irish goddess, Brigid, of the Tuatha Dé Danann; who is a triple goddess. The constellation of Cygnus the Swan is situated upon the Milky Way, close to Cassiopeia, the Queen of Heaven. The triskelion represents the centre-point too –

as the three spirals of energy manifest in equal flow from the one source.

Cygnus the Swan is one of three bird constellations that form an asterism known as the Summer Triangle (the other two birds being Aquila and Lyra). The three swans on Brighid's shield are also a nod to the Summer Triangle, which in Brythonic (Welsh) lore are remembered as the 'Adar Rhiannon' (Bird's of Rhiannon) the divine sovereignty Bride of Dyfed (south west Wales and St Brides Bay).

The big bright star, by the little bear's bottom (and aligned with Brighid's own central axis) represents the pole star, Polaris (of the Little Bear) - around which all other constellations appear to rotate.

* * *

~ THE UNIVERSAL PRAYER OF GRATITUDE ~

I give thanks to The Great Spirit
And to all infinite spirits
Of every direction;
Every star,
And every nucleus of every atom.

I give thanks
To the great expanses of space
Between all things,
That allow all things
To move and to grow.

I give thanks
To the great entanglement,
With the knowledge that,
No matter how far apart
Things may appear to be,
All things are connected.

I give thanks to my Muse
And to my Spirit Guides.
I give thanks to every living creature
For sharing existence with me.
I give thanks to all of the ancestors
For leading the way.

And above all things,
I give thanks to the Mother of All Things
From whom all things were born into being
And to whom
All things will return.

MEMBERS GALLERY

OGHAM CRAFTS

~ IN MEMORY ~
of
RICHARD FOGELBERG

I was very saddened to hear of the death of Richard Fogelberg in February 2021; he actually passed over to the Summerlands around Imbolc, and I am sure that Brighid embraced him with her maternal mantle and warmed him beside her hearth-fire.

Richard (also known as Forest Oak amongst his Druid friends – The Druids of Nwyfrc) was an Ogham Crafts contributor to volume one of *Voices From The Grove*; and he was an enthusiastic encourager of The Ogham Grove, Facebook group, during its early days. I am very grateful.

I was fortunate enough to meet Richard in the real world, all be it briefly. He visited Glastonbury to take part in one of the Glastonbury Dragons celebration days. The photo above was taken at Beltane 2018 and I am almost upon his shoulder – carrying (from the inside) the head of the White Dragon. The Dragon days are always very busy but Richard and I did find time to chat and have a Beltane hug. I am very sad for all of his friends and family. Much love.

SPIRIT NEVER DIES

* * *

~ MARY ELLEN ~
Raffia Weaving

Weaving work in progress

Mary's raffia weavings are inspired by her love for trees and the natural world. **She writes** ~ I think the circle one links to the Ogham the best. Last summer I sat in the meadow near my house by the ancient Elder tree and Silver Birches and found myself weaving a grass circle which I hung on the Elder as a prayer. It stayed there all summer; and this place became my sacred place. I returned there many evenings to watch the young male deer come to eat. I'm going to repeat this again in May when the grasses are longer and the Elderflowers are out and the Silver Birch leaves are green; and the deer return.

Samples of Mary's woven creations.

Mary has no webpages to promote; she just weaves her designs for the love of it.

Metal castings of Rowan leaves

Various stages of production.

Three sickle blades make a triskelion.

Gordon follows a bardic path and works with stones and metal; inspired by the trees and woodland of Aberdeenshire, Scotland, where he lives. He has a particular fondness for the Rowan tree.

Rowan-handle Sickle, used for candle trimming.

In volume one of *Voices From The Grove* Gordon wrote,

'The rowan, my favourite tree since always, brings joy in its
beauty; scent from its bark could be sniffed as nectar...'

Gordon regularly shares his creative explorations and
adventures on The Ogham Grove, Facebook group.

~ KARA CHAMBERS ~
Textile Artist

Now and then something of pure genius comes along. I first became aware of Kara's work, on The Ogham Grove Facebook group, when I saw this fascinating wheel of Birch twigs stitched to a canvas. I thought it, in itself, to be very beautiful; not realising that it was just a preliminary stage to the incredible 'Container of Dreams' that Kara went on to create.

Kara writes ~ I am a nature based textile artist, endeavouring to convey my joy of the natural world in my art. My work is intuitive, seasonally led, and deeply rooted in my local landscape. I typically use natural finds, old textiles, threads and items which I have collected on my many walks.

The Container of Dreams made by Kara Chambers.

Kara continues ~ I started at the beginning of last year (2020), eco-dyeing with new spring leaves, dyeing with bark, printing, mark-making, and mapping the Silver Birch trees which grow within walking distance of my home. I spent time resting against mossy trunks, dreaming, reading and researching as much as I could about Silver Birch, soaking in its energy. This culminated in making a Silver Birch vessel - a Container of Dreams - which holds a year of living and dreaming with this mother of trees and hopes for the future as we begin a new year (Kara wrote in February), and pioneer a way forward.

The container is made from found birch bark, lined with a vintage cotton that I have patterned with rubbings taken from a Silver Birch trunk. These are stitched with Silver Birch dyed silk and hemp thread. The Silver Birch twiglets were foraged from this winter"s carpet.

Please visit Kara's websites, you will find some very beautiful work there, her Birch Container of Dreams is but a simple taster of her inspired creativity.

www.devonhandmaid.wixsite.com

www.facebook.com/devonhandmaid

~ TIM SMYTH ~
Woodsmith

Ogham set, made of Rowan wood, by Tim Smyth.

The above set of Ogham staves are from Tim's early days of working with wood. He has since gone on to specialise in making beautiful bespoke finger rings and bracelets.

Tim has turned his art into a small business called Hamtun Rustic Woodcraft. 'Hamtun' refers to the modern city of Southampton (south coast of England) which is the nearest city to the New Forest.

He has a Facebook page called Hamtun Rustic Woodcraft and he writes,

Welcome to Hamtun Rustic Woodcraft. Here is the showcase of my ring making inspired by the Ogham, an ancient Celtic writing system with a spiritual link to the native trees of our lands. All my rings are handmade in wood.

www.facebook.com/HamtunWoodcrafts

~ ROGER FRANCIS ~
Wood Carver

Roger's business is called Oblivious Gnome Creations

Here are just a selection of Roger's wonderful wood carvings; which I have taken from his Facebook page. Be sure to check it out as there is much more there to see.

'Oblivious Gnome Creations is a craft business producing beautiful hand made wood carvings from reclaimed wood; also one of a kind hand-felted hats'

www.facebook.com/ObliviousGnomeCreations

All carvings by Roger Francis, the Oblivious Gnome.

~ CONNECTIONS ~

If you are a pagan, ecologically-minded, group, order, coven, lodge, or community, and you are open to new people reaching out to connect with you, you may advertise yourself here for free (whatever country you are based in, this journal is global); just email me at,

yuri13oct@yahoo.co.uk

Based near Glastonbury, Somerset, England.

* * *

Also in the Glastonbury area,
for sacred circles, e-courses, and journeys,

Facebook: **Traditional Avalon Mystery School**
Facebook: **Avalon Ninefold Mystery School**

Email: **avalonsacredpathways99@hotmail.com**

THE DRUIDS OF NWYFRE
Based in Portsmouth, UK

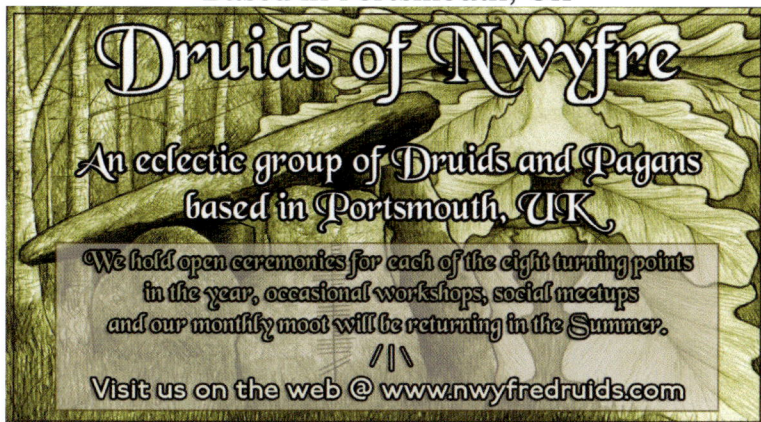

www.nwyfredruids.com
www.stormwatchdruid.uk

WILDWOOD ORDER of ANCIENT DRUIDHISM

The Wildwood Order of Ancient Druidhism would like to welcome anyone interested in working with our Order to contact Deepwood Shenn or Moon Magpie via email:

Wildwood9moonmagpie@yahoo.co.uk.

~ THE OGHAM GROVE ARCHIVES ~

The more we learn the deeper the woods become;
the richer our dreams and visions become,
the stronger our connection to Spirit and Nature becomes.

* * *

The Ogham

Keeping things simple: the Ogham consists of twenty letters.

~ In later centuries five more letters were added, to represent five different extended vowel sounds, but these five extra letters (known as the *Forfeda*) do not appear to have been a part of the original pattern of twenty.

~ In using the Ogham as a divinatory system, similar to the way that Runes are popularly used, some people use twenty Oghams and some people use twenty-five. There is no right or wrong way; it is simply a matter of personal preference. Some people even have more than twenty-five twigs in their pouch because they add extra trees and shrubs that are meaningful to them and the land they live in.

The Ogham Grove

The Ogham Grove is created by placing the twenty letters of the Ogham, in their traditional (Medieval) sequence, evenly-spaced around the circumference of a circle.

~ See the broad golden circle in the image opposite.

~ A circle consists of 360 degrees; dividing that by 20 means that each Ogham letter, or tree, stands 18 degrees apart.

The Patterns of Five

The original twenty letters of the Ogham are divided into four groups of five (known as *aicme*, which is an Irish word that simply means a set, or a group, of things); each letter has a value of one to five (it is all about fives).

~ The number five is very important, as shall be seen, and this number (sacred to the planet Venus and Natural Magic) is to be found in The Ogham Grove in many interesting ways.

~ Every eight years Venus, with her orbital dance between the Sun and the Earth, creates a pentagram in the heavens.

~ The Ogham Grove conceals four interlaced pentagrams (4 x 5) and the two primary pentagrams are illustrated in the design on the opposite page; one is dark green (the Evergreen Pentagram) and the other is golden (The Rose Family Pentagram).

The Ogham Grove

The 1s and 4s add up to 5, the 2s and 3s add up to 5;
and the 5s are complete in themselves.

The ancient Zodiac of Dendera defines the same pattern.

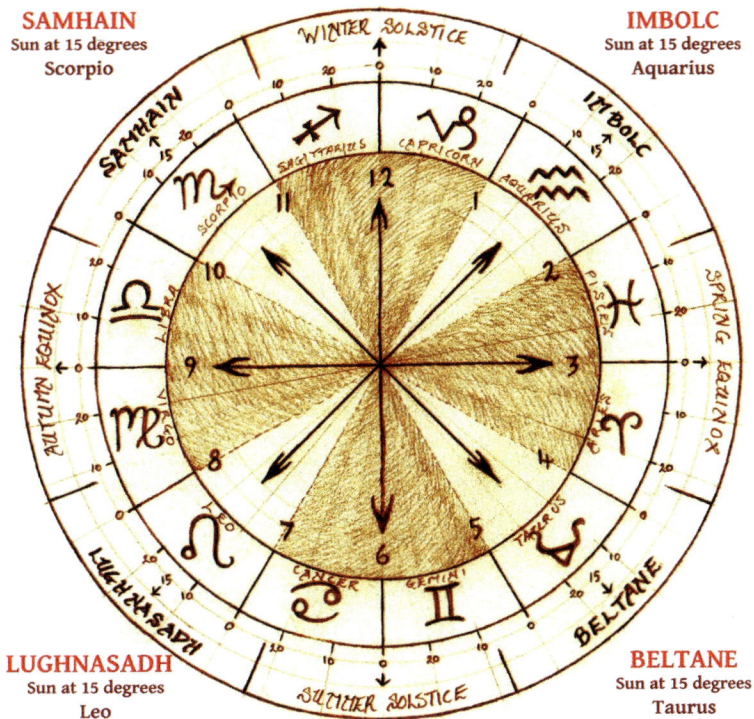

SAMHAIN
Sun at 15 degrees
Scorpio

IMBOLC
Sun at 15 degrees
Aquarius

LUGHNASADH
Sun at 15 degrees
Leo

BELTANE
Sun at 15 degrees
Taurus

It is quite easy to see that the original twenty letters of the Ogham, and their numerical values (notches of one to five), clearly represent the eight festivals of the year when placed in a circle. This mathematical formula is as perfect as Pi.

~ It is not known for certain, whether the Ogham letters originally represented individual trees or not, but this does not negate the year wheel formula of the Ogham's Patterns of Five.

~ We know that the Celts used circles in their art, Druids taught in wooded groves, and the people lived in round houses; it is a perfectly natural thing, to place the Ogham letters in a circle.

~ We also know that the Druids were specifically interested in astronomy; the movements of the planets and the stars. Since very ancient times the signs of the zodiac have been used to navigate and measure the passage of time (and there is plenty of evidence in Celtic art and mythology to demonstrate that the Celts observed the constellations). This means that the Ogham's year wheel (the Patterns of Five) also corresponds with the four seasons and the annual rotation of the fixed stars.

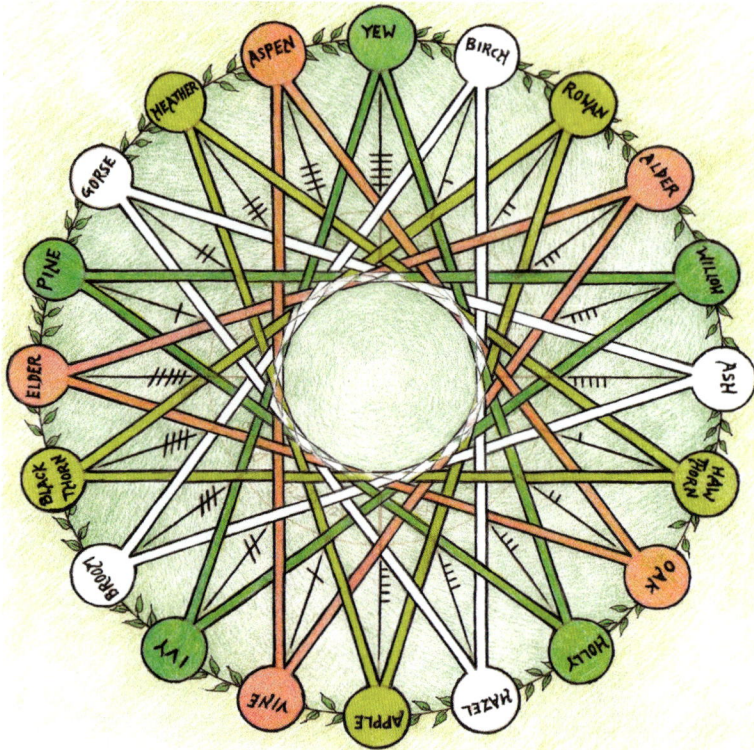

Since Medieval times there has been the notion that each letter of the Ogham corresponds with a tree or shrub; as such, the Ogham is often called the Tree Alphabet.

~ Scholars are of the opinion that the original Ogham letters of the Dark Ages (5th century) are unlikely to have been named after trees and shrubs; which is a scholarly debate to be aware of. However, the tree correspondences have existed since at least the 14th century onward (see *Briatharogam* in the Ogham Glossary).

~ It is not strictly correct to say 'Tree Alphabet' because Vine, Ivy, Broom, Gorse, and Heather, are shrubs rather than trees; but 'Tree Alphabet' is quick and easy to say when chatting casually.

When the Ogham 'trees' are placed within the Ogham year wheel, in their traditional Medieval sequence, many meaningful patterns come to light. The image at the top of this page illustrates the four inter-woven pentagrams of the Ogham year wheel. The dark green pentagram belongs to the evergreen trees and the light green pentagram belongs to the trees of the Rose-family. Governing the evergreen pentagram is the Yew tree, positioned at Winter Solstice, and governing the Rose-family pentagram is the Apple tree, positioned at the Summer Solstice; what are the chances of this being a random pattern?

There is even Celtic (Irish) tree-lore that sings about the union of Yew and Apple.

*'About the commencement of the first century of our era, two lovers, Baile mac Buain, an Ulster chieftain, and Ailinn, a Leinster Princess, died suddenly of grief; each having been deceived by false tidings of the other's death. Out of the grave of Baile **a yew tree** presently sprang up; and from the grave of his beloved Ailinn, **an apple tree**. In seven years, the two trees grew large, with leafy heads bearing a resemblance to the two lovers whose graves were over-shadowed. They were then cut down by the poets, and each was made into a tablet (tabhall filedh). In one were written the Visions, and the Espousals, and the Loves, and the Courtships of Ulster: in the other tales of like import relating to the kingdom of Leinster. In the time of Art, King of Ireland, that is, about a hundred and fifty years afterwards, these tablets, being brought face to face, flew towards each other of their own accord, and **became joined so firmly that they could not be separated.** They were thenceforth preserved amongst the precious things kept in the treasury at Tara, till the palace was burned in the year 241.'*

As well as the hidden pentagrams, there are many other fascinating patterns to be found in the Ogham Grove; for instance, Oak and Holly are positioned on either side of Beltane, the fire festival that traditionally celebrates the seasonal battle between the Oak King and the Holly King attempting to win the hand of the May Queen (Hawthorn) as their bride – all three Trees stand side by side in the Ogham Grove.

The Beltane Three
Beltane is the cusp between Oak and Holly.

So, regardless of whether the original 5th century Ogham letters actually represented trees and shrubs or not, the tree correspondences of the traditional sequence of the Medieval *Briatharogam* (when applied to the Ogham year wheel) do create a very rich cauldron of inspiration.

The Ogham Grove Facebook Group exists for the mutual sharing of insights and ideas about the many patterns discovered and those yet to be discovered. There is also a FILES section in the group, with pdf files of different topics that can be downloaded for free.

How does one use all of this information? That's the topic of the next section of the Ogham Grove Archive.

Gathering your own Ogham Grove; using it for readings; connecting with your land; making it your own; working with it as a Shamanic Threshold.

My first Ogham set. Each twig is about four inches in length and gathered from its correct species of tree. I can hold them all in one fist and they fit nicely into a small cloth pouch; which means that I can take my sacred grove with me wherever I go.

The most popular use of the Ogham, in the present day, is as a tool for divination; for making readings in a way that is very similar to the popular use of Runes. Few people use the Ogham as a writing system anymore (apart from the most dedicated of Celtic crafts people and magical talisman makers). Whilst using the Ogham as a divinatory tool is a perfectly valid thing to do, the Ogham Grove can be so much more than that (as I'll explain) but first let us look at the Ogham as a divinatory system as that is a good place to begin.

Ogham	Letter	Group
	B	
	L	**The 'B Group'**
	F	gesturing to the right
	S	
	N	
	H	
	D	**The 'H Group'**
	T	gesturing to the left
	C	
	Q	
	M	
	G	**The 'M Group'**
	NG	gesturing diagonally
	ST	
	R	
	A	
	O	**The 'A Group'**
	U	gesturing horizontally
	E	
	I	

As with the Runes, the Ogham is an alphabet system, and for divinationary purposes each letter can represent various esoteric and philosophical meanings. Take Birch for instance, its Gaelic name is *Beithe*, it is the letter B, it corresponds with 'New Beginnings', pioneering outlooks, the goddess Elen, and all species of deer ~ but what that might mean in a reading is down to the empathy of the reader.

There are now plenty of books on the market, to tell you what each Ogham letter means in a reading; and they are all valid and logical to the author of each book. Beginners need to explore things for themselves because learning is a journey of finding out what does, and does not, resonate with you. My intention here is to encourage people to gather their own Ogham sets rather than to purchase ready-made ones.

I know that not everybody will have the time, or the willingness, to gather their own Ogham sets, and that they are perfectly happy using a ready-made set; but I believe that gathering your own Ogham is a very important, sacred and magical, thing to do.

Mid gathering, set not yet complete, somewhere in the heart of Wales.

In contradiction to my above statements I have made, and sold, ready-made Ogham sets to many people; because not everybody is very good at arts and crafts, and beautiful workmanship (art) is something to be treasured; and some people like collecting things like owning lots or Tarot decks. So, there is always a place for crafts people to sell their skills; beauty is worth creating for beauty's sake. However, an Ogham set made by somebody else will never be as spiritually profound as a set that you have gradually gathered, one twig at a time, for yourself; because the act of gathering is a sacred pilgrimage that leads on to deeper Ogham magic – as it creates a personal connection with the spirits of Nature (a thing that just cannot be purchased).

A ready-made Ogham set is okay for doing readings, and it may even help you to remember each letter-symbol of the *Beth-luis-nin* (the Ogham alphabet), but then what?

Well, even with a ready-made Ogham set, you could lay your twigs out to create a sacred circle; large enough for you to sit, stand, or meditate within. Begin by placing Yew in the north and Apple in the south, then Ash in the east and Elder in the west – the rest of your Ogham twigs are then easy to fit into their correct places. Now you can work within your own, portable, sacred grove; you can set up this sacred circle anywhere. Do you want to really blow-your-socks-off? Each tree corresponds with a god or goddess from the Celtic pantheons; so you can now be surrounded by the altars of twenty Celtic deities; what are you going to do about that?

The potential is very exciting isn't it? And already, the Ogham becomes so much more meaningful than simply being a tool for doing readings. If you take the time to learn which deity corresponds with each tree (for you specifically, because there is no dogma here) then you can start working with the Ogham on the inner realms.

So far so good, and all of the above can be achieved with a ready-made Ogham set. However, if you gather your own Ogham twigs then greater depths of spiritual connection can be achieved. For instance, when sitting within your own-gathered Ogham Grove, you are surrounded by twenty esoteric portals (doorways) to the twenty locations from whence each of your twigs came from – the parent trees of each of your twigs still exist (hopefully) and they can be reconnected with no matter where you are.

The physical world locations, from whence each of your twigs were gathered from, become an extended part of your own Ogham Grove. When you work within your circle you are then surrounded by twenty doorways to twenty physical world locations. For example, my Heather is from a specific location in the Channel Islands (which are situated in the English Channel between Brittany and Cornwall) and my Gorse is from a humble place that is special to me in Cornwall. My Apple is from Glastonbury; and so on. This amazing concept means that whilst thousands of people may have Ogham Groves, each person's Ogham Grove is a completely unique hub of twenty different sacred places.

You could use this journal to start gathering your twigs (gathering them at their correct time of year); you could use the chart below to record where each of your twigs has come from (as time goes by it can become difficult to remember).

THE OGHAM GROVE
TWENTY TREE SPIRITS & TWENTY SACRED SITES

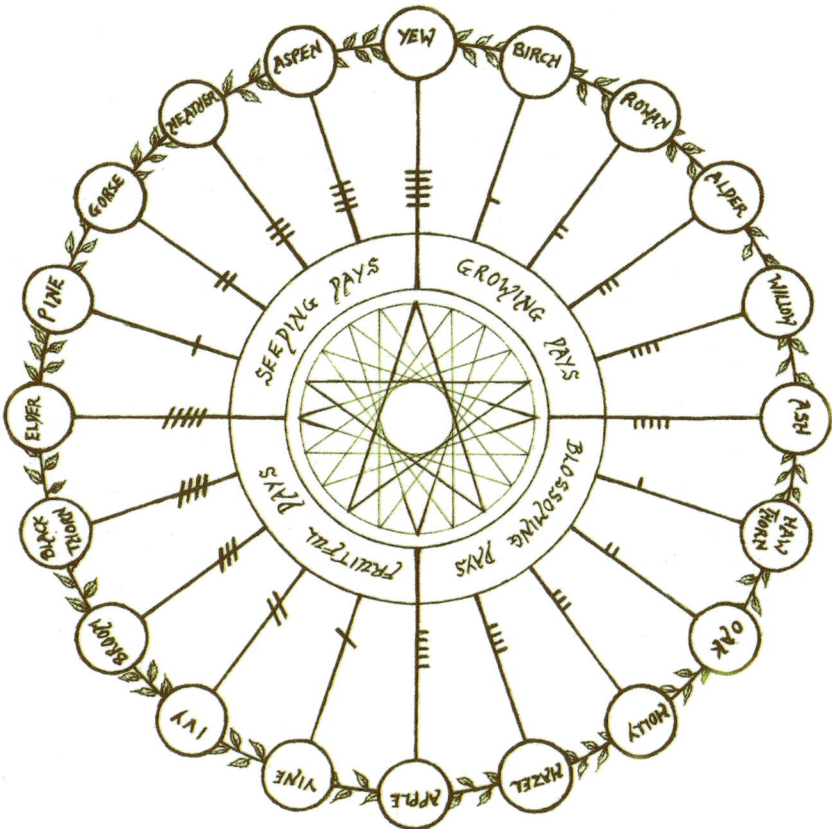

YEW ~ WINTER SOLSTICE ~ NORTH ~ NIGHT
ASH ~ SPRING EQUINOX ~ EAST ~ DAWN
APPLE ~ SUMMER SOLSTICE ~ SOUTH ~ DAY
ELDER ~ AUTUMN EQUINOX ~ WEST ~ DUSK

Your twenty locations could be anywhere; from the trees growing near famous sacred sites, or national parks, to the humble playgrounds and gardens of your childhood. They could all be from the immediate area where you live, or from lots of different countries; it is your Ogham Grove. Follow your instincts and listen to your heart. Which places feel right to you? The places must resonate with your heart and soul.

Whilst it is perfectly possible to gather twigs from lots of different countries, I do think that it is very important to make a connection with the land (and the spirits of the land) wherever you may be living. This becomes an extra challenge for people who live far away from the Ogham's Celtic heartland of Ireland and the western coast (Irish Sea) of the British Isles.

Connecting with the land where you live

One issue that very quickly came to my attention on the Ogham Grove, Facebook group, was that many members that were living in countries far away from the British Isles could not find all of the Ogham trees growing in their lands; so they then had the dilemma of choosing between getting twigs sent to them or finding a native species to substitute the trees they could not find. And things become even more complicated because in the Ogham Grove the twenty trees correspond with specific times of the year but in Australia (and other southern hemisphere countries) when it is Winter Solstice in the Celtic heartlands it is Summer Solstice 'down south' (and Beltane becomes Samhain... or it appears too). So what is to be done?

Well, first of all, the individual must always do what feels right to them; but I would gather twigs from the land that I was living upon - in an attempt to connect with the spirits of that place.

The Ancestral Grove ~ I would do my best to be true to the original twenty trees of the medieval *Bethluisnin*, as a way of honouring the cultural ancestral roots of the system, but then I would look for native trees that were suitable as substitutes for the trees that were missing.

Exotic Ogham Groves of Other Lands ~ So how does one know which 'foreign' trees to use as substitutes? There lies the challenge and the adventure ahead. The answer to which is way beyond my knowledge bank but that is where the Ogham Grove, Facebook group, really comes into its own. For instance, some group members from North America decided that Cottonwood trees were a good substitute for Aspen (and then they discovered that both Cottonwood and Aspen were actually members of the *populus* genus of trees; and that they both have five-pointed stars running through their twigs).

Stars within Aspen

Your Ogham Grove as a Shamanic Threshold

When you gather your own Ogham Grove together, by default, you will be establishing a unique connection with twenty trees and twenty meaningful locations; but more than this, you will be constructing an astral grove within the mind-scape of your psyche. Your own, internalised Ogham Grove, can then be used as a psychic realm that you can consciously visit (and walk around, within your minds-eye) and use as your Shamanic Threshold – the starting point, and first base, of all manner of shamanic journeys and path-workings. So, you can now see, that the potential of the Ogham is so much more than just that as a tool for doing readings. It is a key to the door, that leads on to the Celtic Otherworld; but first you need to gather your sticks, and that should be done mindfully and without too much haste. Take your time, let your garden grow.

Because I have spent many years now, working mindfully within my own Ogham Grove, I can close my eyes and walk around it with ease. I can sit with my back resting against the trunk of my Apple tree and stare across my grove to my Yew tree. I know Hazel is to my right and Vine is to my left. Whether I go for a walk clockwise, or anticlockwise, I can touch, smell, and feel each of my trees. And in the centre of my Grove I have other trees growing (which are private to me and my own journey; you'll have your private ones too). Every tree in my Ogham Grove is a portal to a different place. Every tree is sacred to a god or goddess, and they are all living altars and contact points. Every deity has a sacred animal; and so my Grove can become an entire zoo sometimes. Each tree can be used to climb upwards, ascending to the Upper World, or to follow its roots down to the Lower World. All this from a bunch of twigs – now the Druidic journey can really begin; by developing the inner connection with the ancient stories of ancestral wisdom.

And when the Awen flows, and one's creativity is inspired, then so many games can be played in one's secret garden.

Each tree leads to a different place. One of those places could be your Field of Dreams; a place where you can go to consciously construct, and sew, the imaginal seeds of the things that you would like to attract into your life. Another tree could lead you to your Wise Elder; a place where you can take your troubled mind and seek wise advice. These are just a couple of ideas, and you will come up with ideas of your own. Which tree leads to your Field of Dreams? Which tree leads to your Wise Elder? Where do your other trees take you?

Or, more simply, your Ogham Grove can be your place to go to, to silence your mind and ease a troubled heart. It is your Ogham Grove, your inner sanctum, your sanctuary. A bunch of magic twigs.

~ BRANCHES OF TREE-LORE ~

Buddha gained enlightenment whilst sitting under a tree; the Bodhi Tree, the 'Tree of Awakening'. To the ancient Sumerians of Mesopotamia, the cedar forests of Mount Lebanon were known as 'The Abode of the Gods'. The Phoenicians, great star-watchers and navigators, built their ships from the cedars of Lebanon; and they established the vast sea-trading empire upon which the Celtic sea-trade eventually evolved. The Ogham probably began as a way of recording merchant trading agreements. Gaelic tradition clearly acknowledges that Ireland was, from the beginning, inhabited by sea-faring people from far-away lands; as is recorded in the *Lebor Gabála Érenn* (The Book of Invasions).

The Celtic Sea Trade

GAELS — Brigantes
BRITONS — Demetae, Silures, Catuvellauni, Dobunni, Cantiaci, Durotriges, Dumnonii
Belgae, Atrebates, Caleti, Lexovii, Venelli
THE CELTIC SEA
Osismi, Coriosolites, Veneti, Pictones
GAULS

From Adam and Eve, and their unhappy story with the forbidden Tree of Knowledge in the Garden of Eden; to Odin hanging upon the World Tree, Yggdrasil, seeking to gain the enlightenment of the Runes; to the fae Dryads of ancient Greece and the Yakshinis (female tree-spirits) of India; the esoteric lore of trees has permeated every single culture and mythology of planet Earth. It is not possible to cover all of the known lore in this archive, rather, this essay is about the many 'branches' of tree-lore that can be explored.

The various branches of tree-lore are especially important to people that are intending to create Ogham Groves in other countries; that require substituting the traditional Ogham trees with native alternatives. Logically, and ideally, the substitute trees should have similar tree-lore to the ones that they are replacing. That said, there are no rules on how to choose a substitute tree. These branches are simply logical categories to help the individual along their way. At the end of the day you should always go with what feels right to you; trust your instincts, it is your Ogham Grove.

KINDRED SPECIES - the most natural approach to finding a substitute tree is to look for one of the same species. Take the Willow tree for example, there are actually over three-hundred varieties of Willow alone. As far as the British Isles are concerned (and thus the traditional Ogham) the most common are White Willow and Crack Willow. These days, however, one of the most popular Willows to be found in British gardens and parks is the Weeping Willow (which is actually a hybrid created from White Willow and Chinese Weeping Willow). There are over six-hundred varieties of Oak in the world. So, although it may be difficult to find all twenty traditional Ogham trees in your country, with a bit of research you should be able to find kindred trees of the same species; like Cottonwood being a good substitute for Aspen because they are both members of the poplar family.

NATURE AND HABITAT - if you cannot find a substitute tree of the same species then finding a tree of a similar nature may feel right to you. For instance, Alder and Willow are both water-loving trees and they are usually found near streams, rivers, lakes, and pools; so the water-loving trees of other lands could be suitable as replacements because they belong to the same type of habitat. The first distinguishing difference between trees is that some of them are evergreens (they keep their foliage all year round) and the others are deciduous (they drop their old leaves every autumn to grow new ones in the spring); obviously it would only seem natural, to substitute an evergreen tree with another type of evergreen. Pine is an evergreen, and it is conifer (which simply means that it has cones) but not all evergreens have cones (Holly and Ivy, for instance, have berries) so it may be more appropriate to substitute Pine with another conifer.

THE CYCLE OF THE SEASONS - another perspective that one can look at, in the Ogham Grove, is that the four *aicme* of the Ogham represent the four seasons of the year; which is fine but the northern and southern hemisphere's have polar-opposite seasons.

The Northern Hemisphere Cycle of the Seasons

The B Group ~ The Growing Days
(Birch, Rowan, Alder, Willow, and Ash)
The H Group ~ The Blossoming Days
(Hawthorn, Oak, Holly, Hazel, and Apple)
The M Group ~ The Fruitful Days
(Vine, Ivy, Broom, Blackthorn, and Elder)
The A Group ~ The Seeding Days
(Pine, Gorse, Heather, Aspen, and Yew)

As the southern hemisphere seasons are six months forward (or behind?) its seasonal cycle looks like this,

The Southern Hemisphere Cycle of the Seasons

The Growing Days ~ would be the M Group
(Vine, Ivy, Broom, Blackthorn, and Elder)
The Blossoming Days ~ would be the A Group
(Pine, Gorse, Heather, Aspen, and Yew)
The Fruitful Days ~ would be the B Group
(Birch, Rowan, Alder, Willow, and Ash)
The Seeding Days ~ would be the H Group
(Hawthorn, Oak, Holly, Hazel, and Apple)

Which just doesn't feel right to me. So the Ogham cycle of the seasons may not work in a satisfactory way for many people that are living in the southern hemisphere. However, there is an alternative perspective available, that of observing the annual cycle of the stars (which can be simplified as 'the zodiac') because, regardless of the northern and southern hemispheres having Summer Solstice when the other has Winter Solstice, the astrological alignments of the Ogham Grove are constant for the entire planet. As our mother-ship, planet Earth, orbits around the Sun, the optical illusion of the Sun moving through each sign of the zodiac is created; and it is a perfect year clock and always has been. Instead of the twelve subjective months of the current, Gregorian, calendar system (of some months having 31 days, some having 30, and February having 28 days but 29 every fourth year) the zodiac divides the year into twelve perfect sections (each being 30 degrees wide).

It can take a while for many people to get a good grasp upon esoteric astronomy (the Druids were dedicated to it and the Bardic Mysteries are full of it); but doing so is important because the trees of the Ogham are fixed upon the zodiacal ecliptic path of the Sun (with the only difference being that the zodiac divides the ecliptic into twelve equal sections and the Ogham divides it into twenty). Whether you live in the southern hemisphere or the northern hemisphere, when the Sun is in Virgo, the Sun is in Virgo because our mother-ship (planet Earth) is passing through the thirty degrees of Pisces (which is directly opposite Virgo). So, no matter which hemisphere you live in, when the Sun is in the 18 degrees of Apple, it is in the 18 degrees of Apple because planet Earth is passing through the 18 degrees of Yew; it is to do with the Earth's orbit around the Sun (regardless of the seasonal differences between the northern and southern hemispheres).

Dividing the Sun's path, the ecliptic, into twelve sections (the zodiac) or twenty sections (the Ogham) is a completely harmonious thing to do; as the image below clearly demonstrates. When placed upon a simple grid the zodiac and the Ogham both define the wheel of the year and the Celtic cross-quarter fire festivals of Imbolc, Beltane, Lughnasadh, and Samhain.

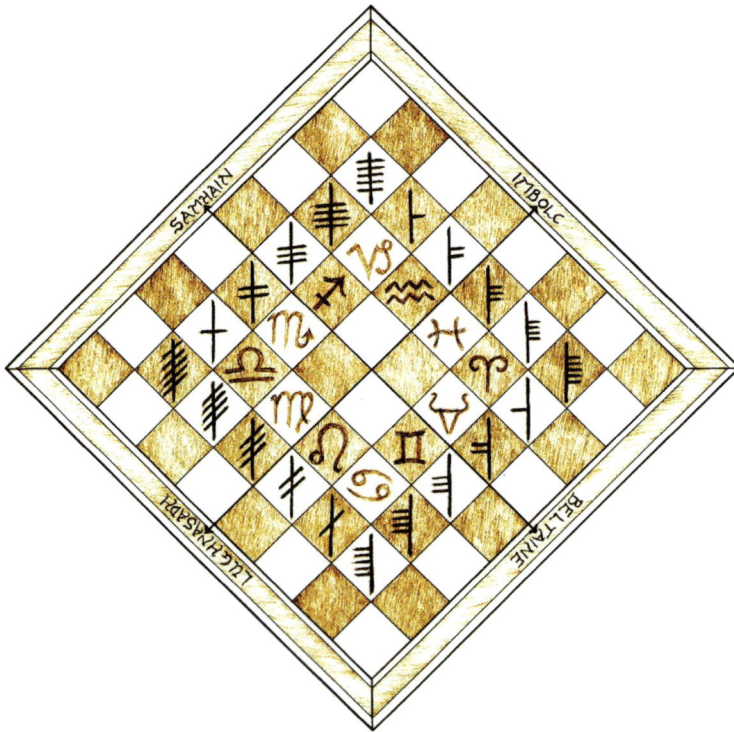

THE STARS AND THE MOON - It would take an entire book to explain the star-lore of all of the trees in the Ogham Grove. The Ogham Grove, Facebook group, is the perfect place for sharing and discussing ideas about star-lore. For the most part, unless you are lucky enough to live in the countryside, the modern world is quite alienated from the starry night. Most people only know about the zodiac signs from fortune-telling, and they would struggle to identify the zodiac constellations shining in the night sky. Electric street-lighting pollutes visibility with a red-orange blur that only the brightest of stars can shine through; but it has not always been that way and our ancestors knew a brighter shining heaven than that of the modern urban world. Since the beginning of time the stars have been the all night, every night, movie cinema of the heavenly kingdom. The constellations represented different gods and goddesses, and the turning of the year sang an eternal song of the spirit world above (and within). Wise Elders used star-lore stories to teach esoteric wisdom to the younger generations. The most well-loved mythologies can be traced back to the annual cyclic movements of the stars; the rediscovery of which is now known as Astro-Archaeology.

The star-lore of the Celts is that of the northern hemisphere, that is just the way it is, there is a big journey of discovery to be made by people living in the southern hemisphere – to learn the star-lore stories of the south and to then apply them to the Ogham year wheel.

There are three primary groups of stars to learn (and this applies to both northern and southern hemispheres), there are the winter stars, the summer stars, and the central stars that are always present – the circumpolar stars. In the northern hemisphere the winter and summer stars are defined by the following patterns.

The Winter Hexagram shines in the night sky during the months of winter and it is formed by six bright stars from the constellations of Orion the Hunter, Canis Major, Canis Minor, Gemini, Auriga, and Taurus the Bull; the dominant image in Brythonic (Welsh) lore is that of Gwyn ap Nudd hunting with his great hound, Dormarth.

The Summer Triangle shines in the night sky during the months of summer and it is formed by three bright stars from the constellations of Cygnus, Aquila, and Lyra; and the traditional image of the Summer Triangle is that of three birds, which in Brythonic (Welsh) lore are known as the *Adar Rhiannon* (the Birds of Rhiannon). Rhiannon herself is the great Queen of Heaven and she corresponds with the circumpolar constellation of Cassiopeia; governing from the centre of The Milky Way.

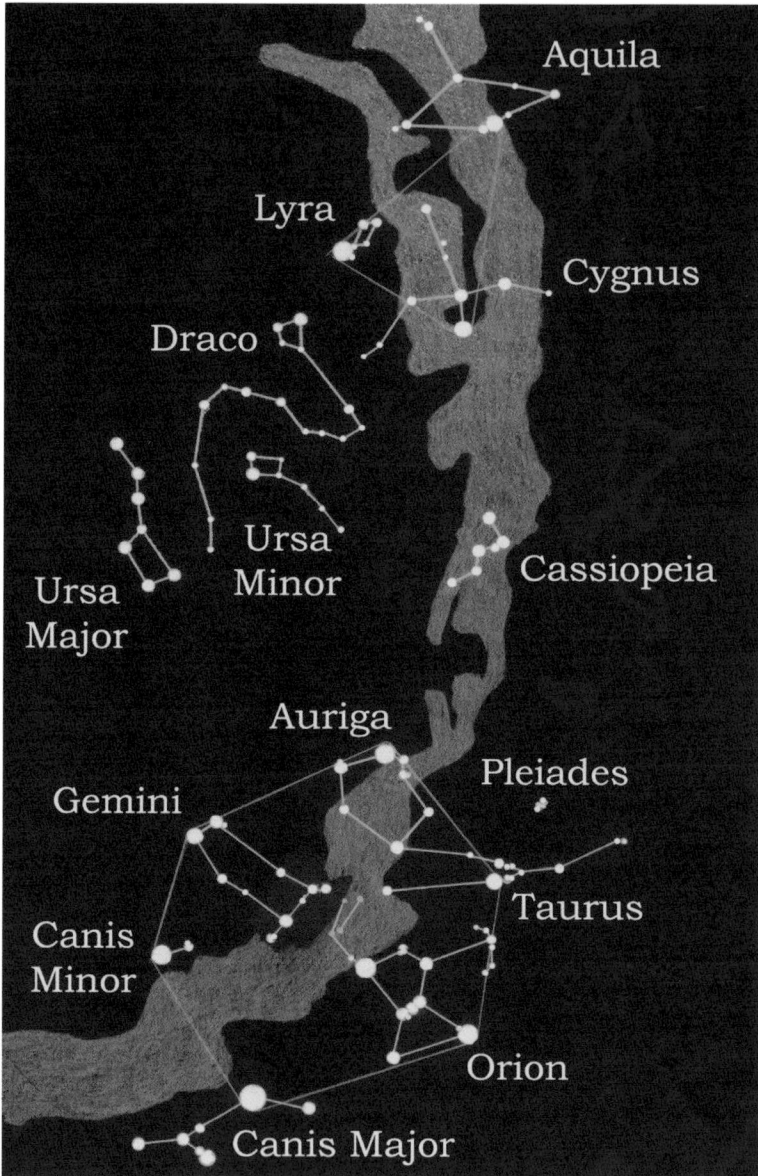

When the Winter Hexagon is in the night sky the Summer Triangle is below the horizon; and vice-versa. This seasonal star-lore is actually depicted upon one of the panels of the Gundestrup Cauldron – where the Queen of Heaven holds a small bird (Lyra) in her upraised hand and two large birds are depicted upon either side of her (Cygnus and Aquila).

As the Summer Triangle is thus illustrated as being raised up, the Hunter and his Hound (Orion and Canis Major, Gwyn ap Nudd and Dormarth) are depicted as being up-side-down (below the horizon) falling down below the Queen of Heaven's stylised breasts. This is very old, pan-European, Celtic star-lore.

The Moon is very important to many magical systems and there is a popular thirteen-month, Ogham-tree, moon calendar; which was invented by the scholar, Robert Graves, in the twentieth century. However, the Ogham always consisted of twenty letters, it was never just thirteen. Some very important trees are missing in the Robert Graves system (Apple and Yew, for instance, the trees of life and death and the Summer Solstice and Winter Solstice, are absent). Moon-lovers need not be disappointed though, as the Moon is a very important part of the Ogham Grove; and it actually visits all twenty trees not just thirteen of them.

Moonlight is reflected sunlight; there is no Moon Magic without the Sun. The Sun visits all twenty trees of the Ogham during the wheel of the year, and the Moon visits all twenty trees every month. The Sun and the Moon are two different wheels, or cogs, of the ever-turning clock of the heavens - but they are different cogs - and one governs the years and the other governs the months.

A year ~ is how long it takes mother-ship, planet Earth, to orbit around the Sun; which creates the optical illusion that the Sun is journeying around the zodiac (and that the Sun is visiting each of the twenty trees of the Ogham).

A month ~ is how long the Moon takes to orbit around planet Earth. There are actually two ways of measuring the Moon's monthly cycle; the Sidereal Month takes 27.32 days and the Synodic Month takes 29.53 days. Both lunar cycles are often approximated to simply '28 days'; but neither *moon-th* fits into a hypothetical thirteen month year wheel (and neither does the approximation of 28 days; although it does come quite close).

13 Sidereal Months (13 x 27.32) = 355.16 days
13 Synodic Months (13 x 29.53) = 383.89 days
28 days 'approximation' (13 x 28) = 364 days

But a year is 365.25 days; so none of the above will fit neatly and over a period of many years the discrepancy becomes ever wider.

It is a lovely idea, a year of lunar months, and many cultures have tried to count the passage of time in that way (there is even a Celtic attempt known as the Coligny Calendar, from Roman Gaul (dating to the 2nd century AD) but all such moon-cycle calendars require a great deal of awkward number-crunching; they are not at all simple and they are of questionable value because agricultural activities are dictated by the weather more than they are by the phases of the moon. What the Moon does is actually very simple; it waxes and wanes. Just as the Sun has two major moments (Winter Solstice and Summer Solstice) so too does the Moon have two major moments (the full moon and the new moon); and it is these two potently magical moments that most people are really interested in. In which tree is the current full moon or new moon? The Sun and the zodiac can teach us this.

A full moon occurs when the Moon is directly opposite the Sun, that is, if the Sun were in the zodiac sign of Capricorn then the full moon would be in the sign of Cancer; because Cancer is directly opposite Capricorn. Therefore, if the Sun were in the 18 degrees of Yew then the full moon would be in the 18 degrees of Apple; because Yew and Apple are directly opposite each other.

A new moon occurs when the Sun and the Moon are conjunct (together in the same zodiac sign); therefore, if the Sun is in Willow then the new moon is also in Willow.

In most traditional Witchcraft and Cunning Magic traditions, it is during the new moon that one's intent is *seeded* (when the Sun and the Moon are 'in bed together') and then the seeded intent gestates as the moon gets bigger and bigger. The full moon is seen as being full-pregnant with that which was seeded during the new moon; and then the Moon returns to sleep with the Sun once again. This insight may help with the Ogham Grove studies. What can be seeded when the new moon is in bed with Oak, or Aspen, or Hawthorn? There is much to explore.

The Ogham Diary in this journal clearly marks the days of new moon and full moon, and there are ten pages at the back of this journal for writing down notes; have some fun.

DIVINE CORRESPONDENCES - Every tree in the Ogham Grove can correspond to a god or goddess; but here there is no dogma and you must choose which deities make the most sense to you. Which gods and goddesses will be honoured in your grove? This in itself is a long journey of discovery but eventually your grove will consist of twenty sacred shrines, as each of your trees becomes an altar and contact-point to your chosen deities.

Mythologically, the Ogham writing system was created by the Celtic mercurial sun-god, Ogma the **Sun-Faced**. He is one of the Tuatha Dé Danann (the gods and goddesses of Ireland), and brother to the goddess Brigid. In classical tradition the most famous sun-god of the zodiac's 'twelve labours' is Hercules; and Ogma is his Celtic counterpart (and he was known as Ogmios in Gaul).

ARCANE ROOTS - Celtic tree-lore has been obscured and hidden in old stories. It can take a long time for English-speaking people to familiarise themselves with the rather strange sounding Celtic names and languages.

Ogma the Sun-Faced
Creator of the Ogham
(which is a solar year wheel system)

Modern English is not the language of Celtic lore. Modern English is derived from Anglo-Saxon and Norman-French; and around ten-thousand Modern English words are actually of French (and Latin) origin.

In the pursuit of rediscovering the lost Celtic tree-lore of the British Isles there are two main Celtic language groups that we can learn from; the Brythonic Celts (Cumbria, Wales, Cornwall, and Brittany) and the Goidelic Celts (Ireland and the Western Isles of Scotland) and the two groups inter-married through the coastal trading network. The Ogham is the writing system of the Goidelic Celts. If the Brythonic Celts had their own writing system there is no surviving evidence for it - under the rule of the Roman Empire the Brythonic Celts had been using Latin for at least three-hundred years before the oldest Ogham pillar-stones first make an appearance.

Whilst the Brythonic Celts may not have had their own tree alphabet, their cultural stories are full of hidden tree-lore; but there is only room here to give a brief glimpse.

Both the Goidelic Celts and the Brythonic Celts played a mysterious chess-like game of strategy - in Irish it is called *Fidchell*, and in Welsh it is called *Gwyddbwyll* - and both names mean exactly same thing, 'Wood Sense'.

Wood Sense can be translated in a number of different ways; for instance, 'Tree-Knowledge', 'Forest-Logic', and even 'Wood-Wise' (as in being Street-wise in urban situations – that is, having your wits about you and knowing your environment). As such, Wood Sense appears to have been a strategy game based in a woodland environment (or it required the players to have knowledge of the trees). The rules of how to play Wood Sense have long been lost and they are now wide open to wild and creative speculation.

Some of my playing pieces, whittled for a *Gwyddbwyll* set.

In Irish tradition the game of *Fidchell* was invented by the ever-young god, brilliant at all things, Lugh Lámfada.   In Welsh tradition it appears to have been connected with the god of Magic and Illusions, Gwydion, the uncle of Lleu Llaw Gyffes (a Brythonic variant of Lugh).

Gwydion is a mercurial trickster god, and scholars have equated him with the Norse god Odin (he who gained the knowledge and wisdom of the Runes whilst hanging in the World

Tree, Yggdrasil). Gwydion's name means 'Born of the Trees' and Tree Magic is his speciality; if any Brythonic deity has Wood-Sense, or Tree-Knowledge, it is he. He created the flower-goddess, Blodeuwedd, out of the flowers of Oak, Broom, and Meadowsweet. There is a poem about Gwydion called *Cad Goddeu* (The Battle of the Trees) and a chess-like game, set in a wooded environment, suggests a battle of the trees; or even trees in battle.

There are many stories about Gwydion and in one of them he animates an entire forest to look as if it is a marching army; he created this illusion to trick his sister, the goddess Arianrhod, into giving her son (Lleu Llaw Gyffes) weapons of empowerment (his rite of passage into manhood).

Lugh Lámfada means 'Lugh of the Long Arm' and Lleu Llaw Gyffes means 'The Fair-haired One of the Skillful Hand'; and they are both variants of the pan-European 'Celtic Mercury' known as Lugus in Gaul. Gwydion created the goddess Blodeuwedd to be the beautiful bride of Lleu Llaw Gyffes (but that turned out badly). The stories of Gwydion portray him as both good and bad, and he shares many similarities with the Arthurian wizard, Merlin. Both Gwydion and Merlin correspond with trees; Gwydion being 'born of the trees' and Merlin living as a wild man in the Caledonian Forest; both are famous wizards, of course, and both used magical trickery to bring divine kings into the world (Lleu Llaw Gyffes and King Arthur – and both divine kingships were doomed to end tragically).

Lugh Lámfada also arranged for the magical animation of trees, to fight against the Fomorians during the Second Battle of Moytura.

"And ye, O Be-cuile and O Dianann," said Lugh to his two witches, "what power can ye wield in the battle?"

"Not hard to tell," said they. "We will enchant the trees and the stones and the sods of the earth, so that they shall become a host under arms against them, and shall rout them in flight with horror and trembling."

This has been but a glimpse at the entwining complexity of the Arcane Roots, but esoteric symbolism need not be so complicated; although the hidden depths are there if you want to search for them – again, The Ogham Grove, Facebook group, is the perfect place for sharing discoveries about arcane lore.

Wild Merlin
by Yuri Leitch

The above image is an illustration of Merlin that I have drawn
for an Arthurian project that I am working on called
The Well Maidens of the Summerlands,
Around Merlin's face I have drawn the foliage of the twenty trees
of the Ogham Grove; in their correct order.

Returning back to the quest of figuring out lore and logic, for substituting trees, the Ogham Grove suggests hidden Arcane Roots of its own. For instance, Gorse and Heather sit side by side (on either side of Samhain) and both shrubs belong to heathland rather than the forest; which implies that the festival of Samhain (and the zodiac sign of Scorpio) corresponds with the untamed expanses of wild moorland and coastal regions (which is actually the perfect terrain for the Wild Hunt) and so a substitute tree should ideally be a shrub that belongs to a similar habitat.

ESSENCES AND MEDICINE - Under the category of Medicine I also include food; and bad food is a poison to our well-being. Your body can only heal itself with the ingredients you choose to give it.

'Let food be thy medicine,
And let medicine be thy food.'
(Hippocrates)

Trees give us a wide variety of nuts and fruits (and even edible leaves like those of the Vine); as well as the more specific medicines like that of Willow-bark being the natural source for Salicin (Aspirin). Everything in nature has a medicinal value of one form or another; and more traditionally this comes under the topic of Herbalism (which was the natural way of medicine, since the dawn of time, until the advent of modern pharmaceutical methods). Almost all of the twenty trees of the Ogham Grove are included in the *Complete Herbal* of Nicholas Culpeper (1616-1654), and those that are not included can be found in more up-to-date modern herbals. You may choose to substitute a tree that has similar medicinal qualities to the tree that you cannot attain. As well as the medicines required to assist the healing processes within the human body there are also the medicines that have a positive effect upon one's mental and emotional health.

The Welsh phrase,
'dod yn ôl at fy nghoed'
meaning,
to return to a balanced state of mind,
literally means,
'to return to my trees'.

Our thoughts effect our health; this is now well understood. Anxiety, fear, and worry, have a detrimental effect upon our digestive systems (which in turn effects our emotional balance). Many decades of negative thinking can even bring about the growth of cancerous tissue within the body. The body only heals when it rests. The body only rests when the mind is peaceful. Time spent with trees can restore inner peace.

Of the Thirty-eight original flower remedies of Dr Edward Bach (1886-1936), nine are trees of the Ogham Grove; and Dr Bach's research equated them with healing certain emotional situations – more research needs to be done to learn the properties of the remaining eleven trees of the Ogham Grove.

The Nine Bach Flower Remedies in the Ogham Grove

Willow ~ to release feelings of resentment
Oak ~ to strengthen those who need endurance
Holly ~ to manage feelings of jealousy and envy
Apple ~ to lift up people with poor self-esteem
Vine ~ helps strengthen those who need to be assertive
Pine ~ to release feelings of guilt
Gorse ~ to alleviate feelings of hopelessness and despair
Heather ~ to let go of destructive self-introspection
Aspen ~ to calm all fears and worries

RESPECTING THE TREES THAT ARE TOO SACRED - Before I say what I am about to say, let me state again that I have no interest in creating any new dogma. My next statement is my own personal and subjective opinion; nothing more. After spending many years contemplating the trees of the Ogham Grove, some very important and sacred trees are (to my mind) screamingly absent - **Beech** (forgetting the forfeda), **Wild Rose,** and **Mistletoe.**

It is very strange to consider any plant-based Druidic calendar, or writing system, ignoring Mistletoe (the most sacred plant of the ancient Druids). Its absence is odd. So too is the absence of the Wild Rose; especially considering that rose-hips have been found Neolithic graves; in the British Isles. Venus, the Rose Queen, is clearly in harmony with many of the Ogham Grove patterns. And Beech, 'the Queen of the Woods', whose groves were sacred to the Moon goddesses, Diana and Artemis; why is she absent from the original sequence of twenty?

Here is my reasoning (and it is only a gut-feeling and nothing more). I think that Beech, Wild Rose, and Mistletoe, are absent because they were considered too sacred to be included. This may sound strange but many years ago, when illustrating the *Sacred Sites Oracle Deck*, I learnt that some cultures considered it a taboo to depict their most sacred divinities. For instance, the Inca people of South America create golden icons of their Sun-god, Inti, but they consider it a taboo to create images of Pacha-Mama, their mother-goddess, because she is too sacred. Do the trees of the Ogham Grove create a circumference, an outer wall that encloses a sacred area? It is up to you.

I think that there is enough information in this archive for the intelligent person to create an Ogham Grove from the native trees anywhere in the world; whether they have the availability of the traditional trees or not. Dividing the year into twenty is all that you need to do; with the trees that have meaningful correspondences that matter to you.

Stakes of Rowan and Alder creating the portal of Imbolc

~ OGHAM GLOSSARY ~

Aicme ~ is an Old Irish word for a group, or a family, of things. The Ogham is divided into four sections and each section is called an aicme – the *aicme Beithe*, the *aicme Uatha*, the *aicme Muin*, and the *aicme Ailm*. It is simply a way of saying 'the B group', 'the H group', and so on. In the Ogham Grove the four aicme also correspond with the four seasons of the year,

The Aicme Beithe incorporates
Imbolc to Spring Equinox ~ the budding time.
The Aicme Uatha incorporates
Beltane to Summer Solstice ~ the blossoming time.
The Aicme Muin incorporates
Lughnasadh to Autumn Equinox ~ the fruiting time.
The Aicme Ailm incorporates
Samhain to Winter Solstice ~ the seeding time.

Ballymote, The Book of (*Leabhar Bhaile an Mhóta*) ~ is a compilation of old Irish manuscripts that were compiled around 1390 AD. Its contents are older than 1390, of course, although they are impossible to date with any accurate certainty. Parts of the compilation are believed to have originated in the 7th century but much of it is thought to have been added in the 12th century. Amongst its pages it contains the only known copy of *The Scholar's Primer* (the *Auraicept na n-Éces*); one of the earliest source manuscripts about Ogham lore, and the origin of each Ogham letter representing individual trees – thus the Ogham Grove tree sequence dates to at least 1390 AD.

Beth-Luis-Nin ~ is the name of the Ogham alphabet. The word 'alphabet' is derived from the first two letters of the Greek writing system, *alpha* and *beta*; and 'bethluisnin' is derived from the first two letters of the Ogham, *beithe* and *luis*.

Some confusion was created by one scholar who assumed that '*nin*' was '*nion*' (Ash tree) and that therefore the *aicme Beithe* sequence should be B-L-N-F-S instead of B-L-F-S-N; and it is presented as such in some books. However, modern scholars now consider '*nin*' as simply being a word-ending; so bethluisnin simply translates as the *beithe-luis* system (just as the alphabet is the *alpha-beta* system).

Bríatharogam ~ is an Old Irish word that translates into English as 'word ogham' (which is a two-word kenning that attempts to explain the meanings of the names of the individual letters of the

Ogham alphabet). There are three known variations,

The Bríatharogam of *Morainn mac Moin* ~ (14th century)
The Bríatharogam of *Maic ind Óc* ~ (14th century)
The Briatharogam of *Con Culainn* ~ (16th century)

The first two Bríatharogam can be found in *The Ogham Tract*. The Bríatharogam are the oldest evidence that the Ogham letters are named after trees (there is no earlier evidence and the Bríatharogam are about 700 years later than the Ogham engraved pillar-stones of the 6th century; and as such, all of the Bríatharogam may be the fancies of a late Medieval bardic tradition that cannot prove to be authentic Dark Age lore... this is a topic of much heated debate among Celtic scholars.

The Ogham writing system dates back to the 4th century but the lore that each letter is a tree can only be traced back to the 14th century). An example of the three versions of the Bríatharogam for Birch (Beithe) now follow,

Morainn mac Moín ~ 'withered foot with fine hair.'
Mac ind Óc ~ 'greyest of skin.'
Con Culainn ~ 'beauty of the eyebrows.'

Upon such meagre information many people attempt to use the Bríatharogam as a way of using the Ogham for readings (like the common use of Runes) and yet the lore of the Birch tree is so much richer, and more profound, than these simple and questionable kennings.

Whilst the Bríatharogam are a late Medieval tradition they do carry the notion of letters representing trees; and they are the source for the traditional sequence of trees that we use in the Ogham Grove (a sequence that dates back to at least 1390 AD).

Brythonic ~ is a northern Celtic language group, and culture, corresponding with the modern Welsh, Cornish, and Breton languages.

Celts ~ Celtic culture covered a vast area of Europe as it spread from the Atlantic Ocean to the Ukraine, in Eastern Europe. The Ogham writing system was created by the Goidelic Celts of Ireland and it was absorbed into the territories of the Brythonic Celts (Scotland, Wales, Cornwall, and Brittany).

Druid ~ is thought to mean something like 'Oak-Knower' or 'Oak-Seer'. The Druids were the spiritual teachers, lawyers, and politicians, of the Celtic people; and the word *Druid* shares a common root with the word *Dryad*.

Dryad ~ originally, specifically referred to the spirit of an Oak tree, but it is now used to refer to all tree-spirits no matter what the species of tree.

Drys (Greek) ~ Oak tree
Dryad (Greek) ~ Oak spirit
Druidés (Greek) ~ Druids
Druidés (Latin) ~ Druids
Drui (Old Irish) ~ Druid
Druw (Old Cornish) ~ Druid
Dryw (Middle Welsh) ~ Druid

Fid (and **Feda**) ~ *Fid* is the Gaelic singular for an Ogham letter, and *Feda* is plural (letters). *Fid/Feda* mean tree/trees; so whilst the specific tree correspondences to the Ogham letters may be debatable, the letters themselves are called trees (*Feda*). There is probably a connection with the mystical game of *Fidchell* (a chess-like game invented by the Celtic god, Lugh).

Fidchell ~ a chess-like game invented by Lugh. *Fidchell* (just like its Welsh equivalent, *Gwyddbwyll*) translates as 'Wood-Sense', 'Tree-Logic', or 'Tree-Wise'. The rules of the game have long been forgotten and in many modern translations of Medieval stories it is often simply translated as 'Chess'; but it was something very different and uniquely Celtic.

Forfeda ~ the *Forfeda* are five additional letters that were added to the Ogham alphabet. They are not of the original sequence of twenty letters and as such they are not significant to the Ogham Grove year wheel; but there is no reason why they could not be sacred trees within the centre of your own Ogham Grove (but that is down to each individual to decide for themselves).

Gaelic ~ is the Celtic language of Ireland and the Western Isles of Scotland (Irish Gaelic and Scots Gaelic vary somewhat but they share the same Old Irish (Goidelic) Celtic root language).

Goidelic ~ is a northern Celtic language group corresponding with the Gaelic language (modern Ireland, Western Scotland, and the Isle of Man).

Gregorian Calendar ~ is the current world calendar system. It was established by Pope Gregory XIII, in 1582, and it is named after him. It replaced the older, Julian Calendar, established by the Roman Empire. The Iron Age Celts, and their Druids, used neither the Roman nor the Catholic calendar systems. Britain did not adopt the use of the Gregorian Calendar until 1742. There were eleven days difference between the two calendar systems which is why 'Old Christmas Day' is on the 6th January (and not December 25th); this eleven day discrepancy also applies to all folk festivals, for instance, Old May Day would happen eleven days after the current Gregorian Calendar's May Day. Beltane has never changed, it is the mid-point between Spring Equinox and Summer Solstice (when the Sun is at the 15th degree of Taurus). The eight stations of the Sun are constant, and they re-calibrate each year with the Winter Solstice.

Julian Calendar ~ was the old calendar system of Europe, before being replaced by the Gregorian Calendar in 1582; it was established in the year 45 BC by the Roman Empire, and it was named after Julius Caesar.

Ogham Tract, The ~ an alternative title for *The Book of Ogams* which in Irish is called, *In Lebor Ogaim*. It is the earliest source of information about the Ogham being a tree alphabet.

Ogma ~ is the Gaelic god of writing and the mythological creator of the Ogham (it is named after him). He is the brother of the goddess, Brigid, and he is a powerful solar-hero of Herculean strength.

Pillar-stones ~ are the most common archaeological evidence of the Ogham writing system. Ogham pillar-stones were used by the Scoti (Gaelic coastal traders and raiders) from the 5th Century onward; to mark their territorial claims and important burials. The Roman Empire retreated from Brittania in 410 AD; from then onward the Scoti began claiming coastal territories along the west coast of Britain (as did the Saxons with their Runes along the east coast of Britain) – interesting times, with the beleaguered Romanised Britons (descendants of the Brythonic Celts) using the Latin alphabet. In the British Isles the Ogham, Latin, and Runic, writing systems all existed at the same time for a short while. There are in Wales examples of bi-lingual pillar-stones, inscribed in both Ogham and Latin (which helped the Ogham writing system to be decoded).

Scoti ~ (also Scotti) is what the Romans called the Gaelic Celts; as such it is a Latin word, and a name that stuck to the Gaelic people of the Western Isles and eventually became the origin of the name Scotland (Land of the Scoti). The Scoti used the Ogham to mark their territories and important burials; about four-hundred Ogham-inscribed pillar-stones still survive.

* * *

* * *

DIARY PAGES

BELTANE 2021
to
BELTANE 2022

Significant dates have been worked out
by UT (Universal Time)
which is akin to GMT.

Reader's days may differ slightly
depending upon one's own time zone.

* * *

DAYS OF OAK
27 degrees Aries
to 15 degrees Taurus
BELTANE

Sat Apr 17	First full day of Oak
Sun Apr 18	
Mon Apr 19	
Tue Apr 20	
Wed Apr 21	
Thu Apr 22	
Fri Apr 23	
Sat Apr 24	
Sun Apr 25	
Mon Apr 26	Full Moon in Gorse

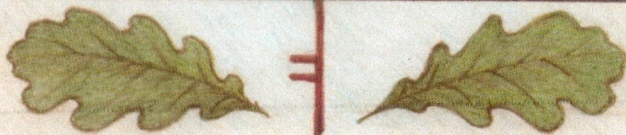

Tue Apr 27

Wed Apr 28

Thu Apr 29

Fri Apr 30

Sat May 1

Sun May 2

Mon May 3

Tue May 4

Wed May 5   Oak to Holly day

BELTANE

OAK
Strength and Endurance

The First Herald of Beltane

DAYS OF HOLLY

BELTANE

15 degrees Taurus
to 3 degrees Gemini

BELTANE

Thu May 6	First full day of Holly
Fri May 7	
Sat May 8	
Sun May 9	
Mon May 10	
Tue May 11	New Moon
Wed May 12	
Thu May 13	
Fri May 14	
Sat May 15	

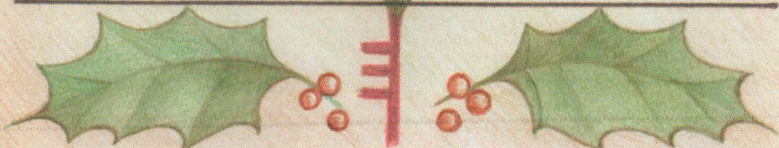

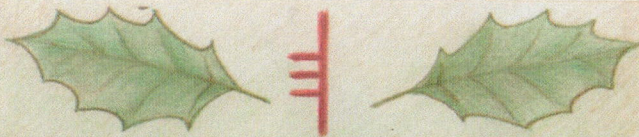

Sun May 16

Mon May 17

Tue May 18

Wed May 19

Thu May 20

Fri May 21

Sat May 22

Sun May 23   Holly to Hazel day

HOLLY
The Immortal Self

The Second Herald of Beltane

DAYS OF HAZEL

3 degrees Gemini
to 21 degrees Gemini

Mon May 24	First full day of Hazel
Tue May 25	
Wed May 26	Full Moon inAspen
Thu May 27	
Fri May 28	
Sat May 29	
Sun May 30	
Mon May 31	
Tue Jun 1	
Wed Jun 2	

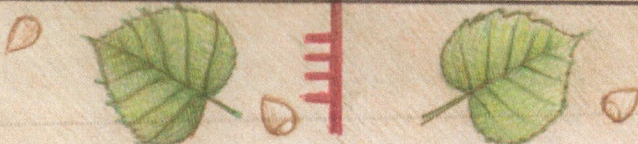

Thu Jun 3

Fri Jun 4

Sat Jun 5

Sun Jun 6

Mon Jun 7

Tue Jun 8

Wed Jun 9

Thu Jun 10 — New Moon

Fri Jun 11 — Hazel to Apple day

HAZEL

Intuition and Inspiration

Warden of the Early Summer

DAYS OF APPLE
21 degrees Gemini
SUMMER SOLSTICE
to 9 degrees Cancer

Sat Jun 12	First full day of Apple
Sun Jun 13	
Mon Jun 14	
Tue Jun 15	
Wed Jun 16	
Thu Jun 17	
Fri Jun 18	
Sat Jun 19	
Sun Jun 20	
Mon Jun 21	**SUMMER SOLSTICE**

Tue Jun 22

Wed Jun 23

Thu Jun 24   Full Moon in Yew

Fri Jun 25

Sat Jun 26

Sun Jun 27

Mon Jun 28

Tue Jun 29

Wed Jun 30   Apple to Vine day

APPLE
Health and Immortality

Guardian of the South

DAYS OF VINE

9 degrees Cancer
to 27 degrees Cancer

Thu Jul 1	First full day of Vine
Fri Jul 2	
Sat Jul 3	
Sun Jul 4	
Mon Jul 5	
Tue Jul 6	
Wed Jul 7	
Thu Jul 8	
Fri Jul 9	New Moon
Sat Jul 10	

Sun Jul 11

Mon Jul 12

Tue Jul 13

Wed Jul 14

Thu Jul 15

Fri Jul 16

Sat Jul 17

Sun Jul 18

Mon Jul 19   Vine to Ivy day

VINE
Relaxing Inhibitions

Pioneer of the Fruitful Days

DAYS OF IVY
27 degrees Cancer
to 15 degrees Leo
LUGHNASADH

Tue Jul 20

Wed Jul 21

Thu Jul 22

Fri Jul 23   Full Moon in Rowan

Sat Jul 24

Sun Jul 25

Mon Jul 26

Tue Jul 27

Wed Jul 28

Thu Jul 29

Fri Jul 30

Sat Jul 31

Sun Aug 1

Mon Aug 2

Tue Aug 3

Wed Aug 4

Thu Aug 5

Fri Aug 6

Sat Aug 7   Ivy to Broom day

LUGHNASADH

IVY
Binding and Unity

The First Herald of Lughnasadh

DAYS OF BROOM

LUGHNASADH

15 degrees Leo
to 3 degrees Virgo

LUGHNASADH

Sun Aug 8	First full day of Broom and New Moon
Mon Aug 9	
Tue Aug 10	
Wed Aug 11	
Thu Aug 12	
Fri Aug 13	
Sat Aug 14	
Sun Aug 15	
Mon Aug 16	
Tue Aug 17	

Wed Aug 18

Thu Aug 19

Fri Aug 20

Sat Aug 21

Sun Aug 22   Full Moon in Alder

Mon Aug 23

Tue Aug 24

Wed Aug 25

Thu Aug 26   Broom to Blackthorn day

BROOM
Perfect Beauty and Freedom

The Second Herald of Lughnasadh

DAYS OF
BLACKTHORN
3 degrees Virgo
to 21 degrees Virgo

Fri Aug 27   First full day of Blackthorn

Sat Aug 28

Sun Aug 29

Mon Aug 30

Tue Aug 31

Wed Sep 1

Thu Sep 2

Fri Sep 3

Sat Sep 4

Sun Sep 5

Mon Sep 6	New Moon
Tue Sep 7	
Wed Sep 8	
Thu Sep 9	
Fri Sep 10	
Sat Sep 11	
Sun Sep 12	
Mon Sep 13	Blackthorn to Elder day

BLACKTHORN

Provisions and Protection

Warden of the Early Autumn

DAYS OF ELDER

21 degrees Virgo
AUTUMN EQUINOX
to 9 degrees Libra

Tue Sep 14	First full day of Elder
Wed Sep 15	
Thu Sep 16	
Fri Sep 17	
Sat Sep 18	
Sun Sep 19	
Mon Sep 20	Full Moon in Ash
Tue Sep 21	
Wed Sep 22	**AUTUMN EQUINOX**
Thu Sep 23	

Fri Sep 24

Sat Sep 25

Sun Sep 26

Mon Sep 27

Tue Sep 28

Wed Sep 29

Thu Sep 30

Fri Oct 1 — Elder to Pine day

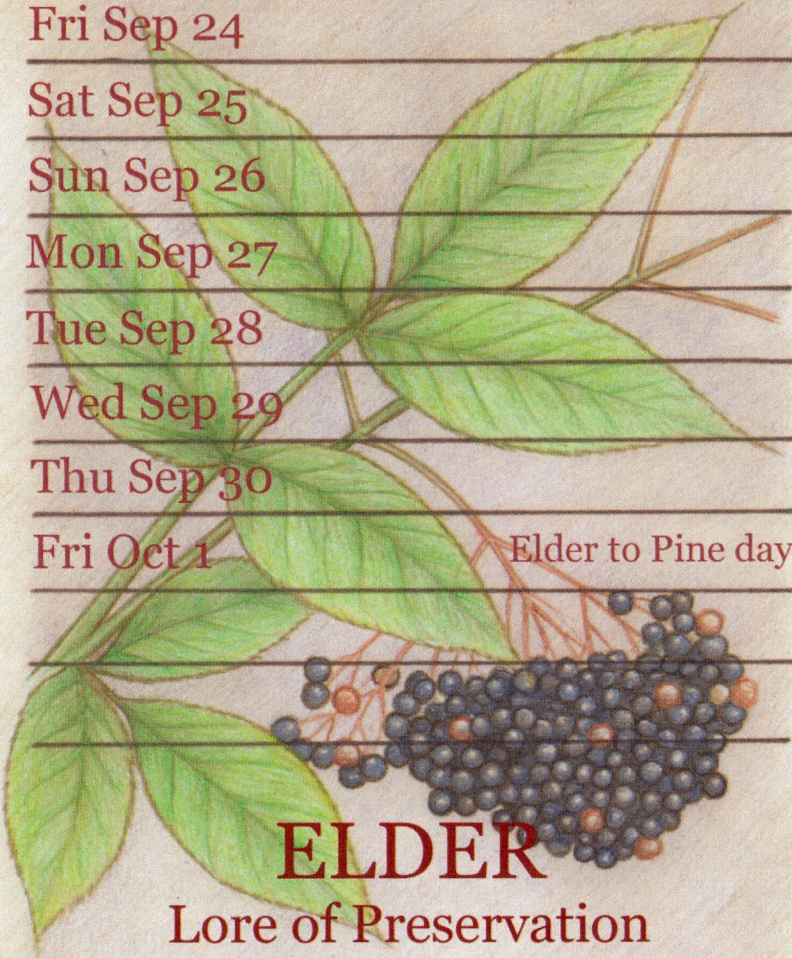

ELDER
Lore of Preservation

Guardian of the West

DAYS OF PINE

9 degrees Libra
to 27 degrees Libra

Sat Oct 2	First full day of Pine
Sun Oct 3	
Mon Oct 4	
Tue Oct 5	
Wed Oct 6	New Moon
Thu Oct 7	
Fri Oct 8	
Sat Oct 9	
Sun Oct 10	
Mon Oct 11	

Tue Oct 12

Wed Oct 13

Thu Oct 14

Fri Oct 15

Sat Oct 16

Sun Oct 17

Mon Oct 18

Tue Oct 19

Wed Oct 20 — Pine to Gorse day and Full Moon in Hawthorn/Oak

PINE
Spiritual Aspirations

Pioneer of the Seeding Days

DAYS OF GORSE
27 degrees Libra
to 15 degrees Scorpio
SAMHAIN

Thu Oct 21 — First full day of Gorse

Fri Oct 22

Sat Oct 23

Sun Oct 24

Mon Oct 25

Tue Oct 26

Wed Oct 27

Thu Oct 28

Fri Oct 29

Sat Oct 30

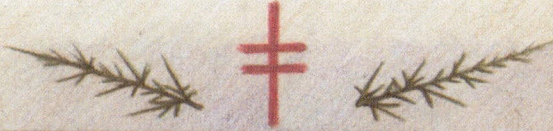

Sun Oct 31

Mon Nov 1

Tue Nov 2

Wed Nov 3

Thu Nov 4   New Moon

Fri Nov 5

Sat Nov 6

Sun Nov 7   Gorse to Heather day

SAMHAIN

GORSE
Shelter from the Storm

The First Herald of Samhain

DAYS OF HEATHER
SAMHAIN
15 degrees Scorpio
to 3 degrees Sagittarius

SAMHAN

Mon Nov 8	First full day of Heather
Tue Nov 9	
Wed Nov 10	
Thu Nov 11	
Fri Nov 12	
Sat Nov 13	
Sun Nov 14	
Mon Nov 15	
Tue Nov 16	
Wed Nov 17	

Thu Nov 18

Fri Nov 19 — Full Moon in Holly

Sat Nov 20

Sun Nov 21

Mon Nov 22

Tue Nov 23

Wed Nov 24

Thu Nov 25 — Heather to Aspen day

HEATHER
Domestic Comforts

The Second Herald of Samhain

DAYS OF ASPEN

3 degrees Sagittarius
to 21 degrees Sagittarius

Fri Nov 26   First full day of Aspen

Sat Nov 27

Sun Nov 28

Mon Nov 29

Tue Nov 30

Wed Dec 1

Thu Dec 2

Fri Dec 3

Sat Dec 4   New Moon

Sun Dec 5

Mon Dec 6

Tue Dec 7

Wed Dec 8

Thu Dec 9

Fri Dec 10

Sat Dec 11

Sun Dec 12   Aspen to Yew day

ASPEN
Facing One's Fears

Warden of the Early Winter

DAYS OF YEW

21 degrees Sagittarius
WINTER SOLSTICE
to 9 degrees Capricorn

Mon Dec 13	First full day of Yew
Tue Dec 14	
Wed Dec 15	
Thu Dec 16	
Fri Dec 17	
Sat Dec 18	Full moon in Apple
Sun Dec 19	
Mon Dec 20	
Tue Dec 21	WINTER SOLSTICE
Wed Dec 22	

Thu Dec 23

Fri Dec 24

Sat Dec 25

Sun Dec 26

Mon Dec 27

Tue Dec 28

Wed Dec 29

Thu Dec 30   Yew to Birch day

YEW
Death and Rebirth

Guardian of the North

DAYS OF BIRCH

9 degrees Capricorn
to 27 degrees Capricorn

Fri Dec 31	First full day of Birch
Sat Jan 1	
Sun Jan 2	New Moon
Mon Jan 3	
Tue Jan 4	
Wed Jan 5	
Thu Jan 6	
Fri Jan 7	
Sat Jan 8	
Sun Jan 9	

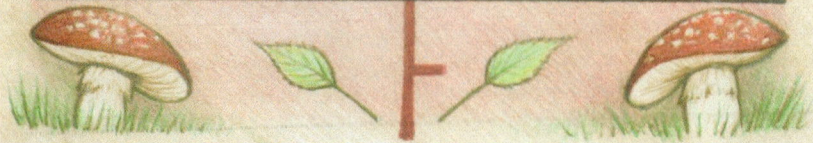

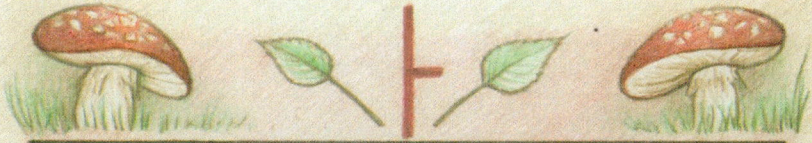

Mon Jan 10

Tue Jan 11

Wed Jan 12

Thu Jan 13

Fri Jan 14

Sat Jan 15

Sun Jan 16

Mon Jan 17   Birch to Rowan day
                  and Full Moon in Vine

BIRCH
New Beginnings

Pioneer of the First Days
of the Year

DAYS OF ROWAN
27 degrees Capricorn
to 15 degrees Aquarius
IMBOLC

Tue Jan 18	First full day of Rowan
Wed Jan 19	
Thu Jan 20	
Fri Jan 21	
Sat Jan 22	
Sun Jan 23	
Mon Jan 24	
Tue Jan 25	
Wed Jan 26	
Thu Jan 27	

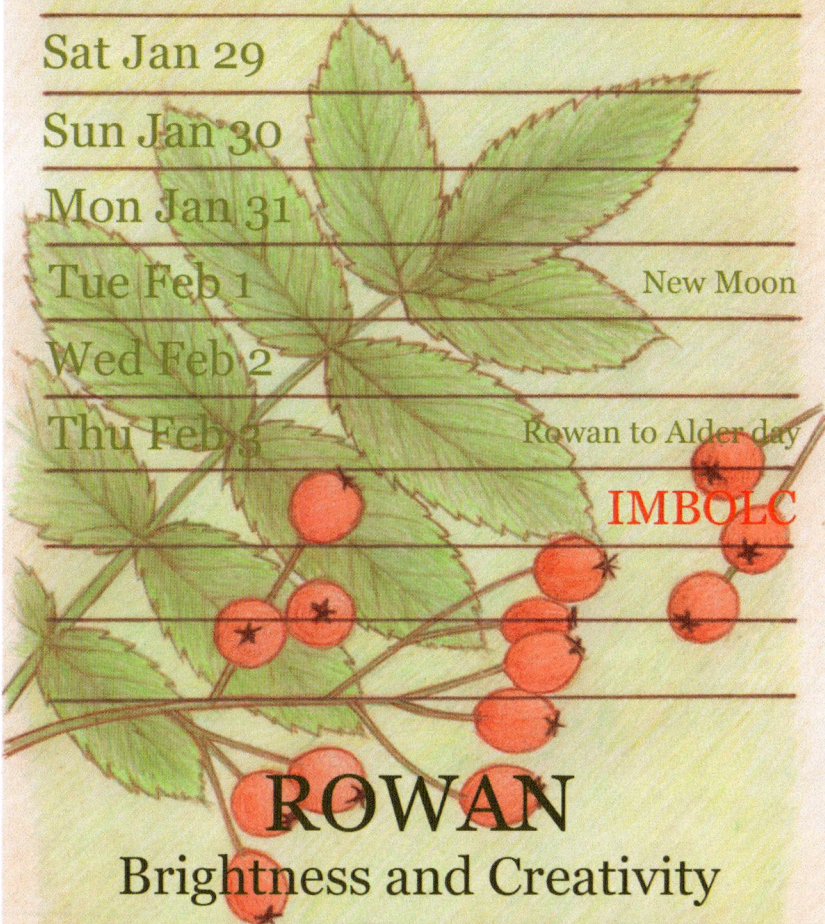

Fri Jan 28

Sat Jan 29

Sun Jan 30

Mon Jan 31

Tue Feb 1 — New Moon

Wed Feb 2

Thu Feb 3 — Rowan to Alder day

IMBOLC

ROWAN

Brightness and Creativity

The First Herald of Imbolc

DAYS OF ALDER

IMBOLC

15 degrees Aquarius
to 3 degrees Pisces

IMBOLC

Fri Feb 4	First full day of Alder
Sat Feb 5	
Sun Feb 6	
Mon Feb 7	
Tue Feb 8	
Wed Feb 9	
Thu Feb 10	
Fri Feb 11	
Sat Feb 12	
Sun Feb 13	

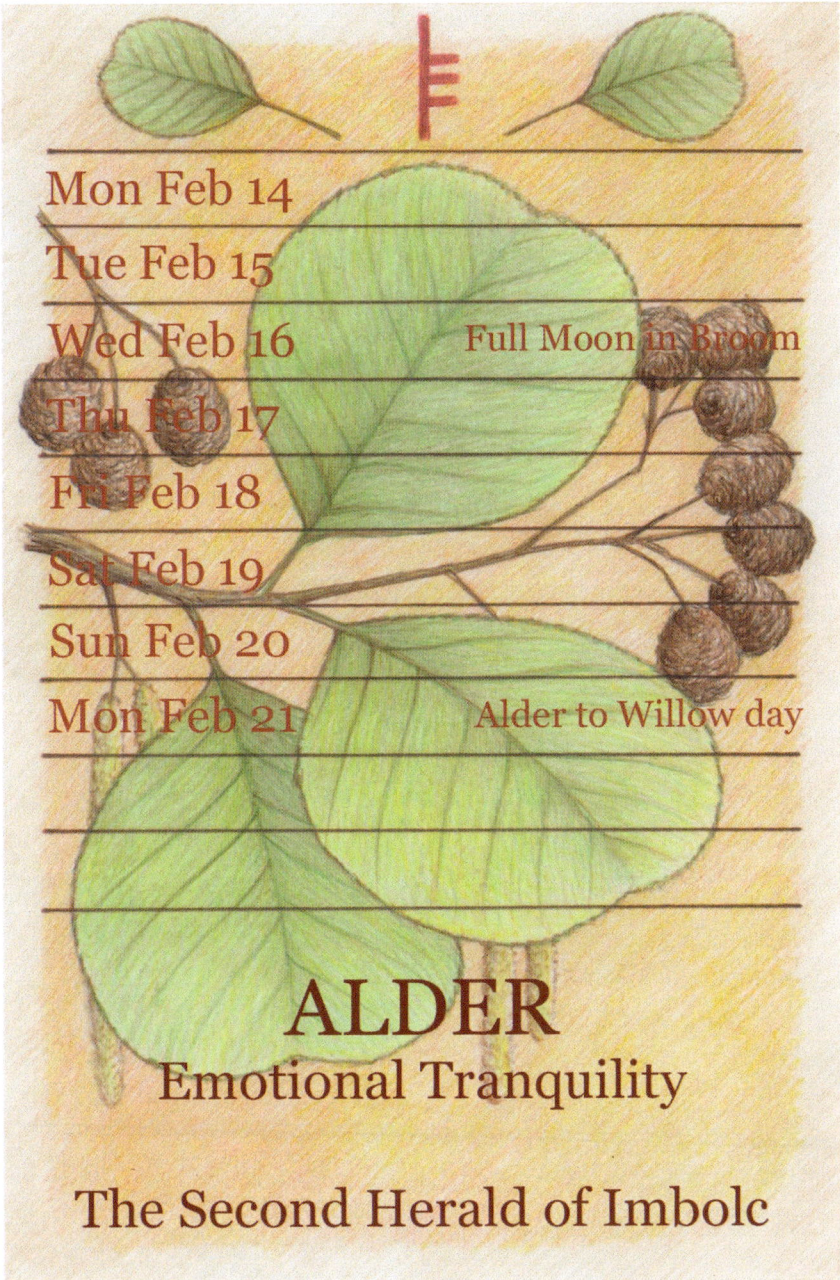

Mon Feb 14

Tue Feb 15

Wed Feb 16   Full Moon in Broom

Thu Feb 17

Fri Feb 18

Sat Feb 19

Sun Feb 20

Mon Feb 21   Alder to Willow day

ALDER
Emotional Tranquility

The Second Herald of Imbolc

DAYS OF WILLOW

3 degrees Pisces
to 21 degrees Pisces

Tue Feb 22	First full day of Willow
Wed Feb 23	
Thu Feb 24	
Fri Feb 25	
Sat Feb 26	
Sun Feb 27	
Mon Feb 28	
Tue Mar 1	
Wed Mar 2	New Moon
Thu Mar 3	

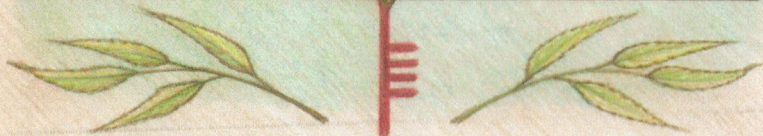

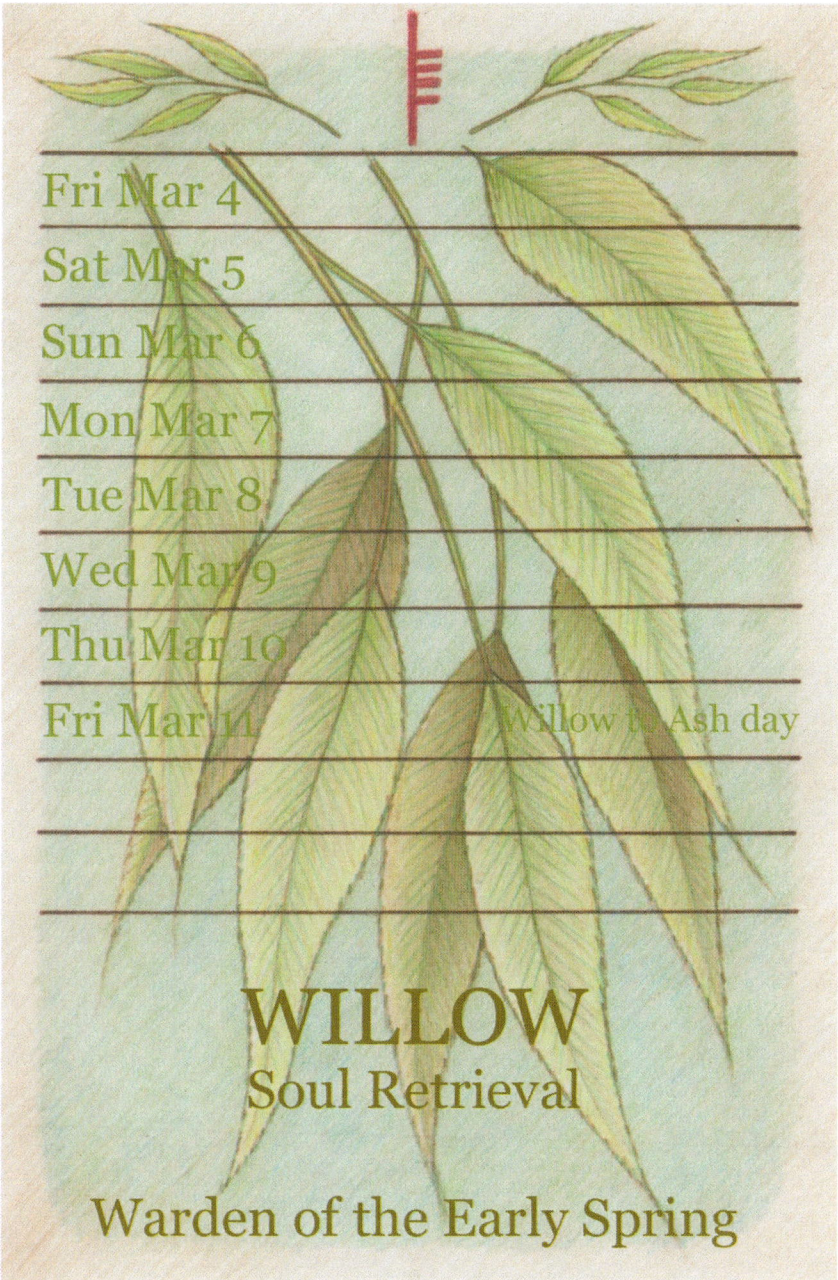

Fri Mar 4

Sat Mar 5

Sun Mar 6

Mon Mar 7

Tue Mar 8

Wed Mar 9

Thu Mar 10

Fri Mar 11   Willow to Ash day

WILLOW
Soul Retrieval

Warden of the Early Spring

DAYS OF ASH

21 degrees Pisces
SPRING EQUINOX
to 9 degrees Aries

Sat Mar 12	First full day of Ash
Sun Mar 13	
Mon Mar 14	
Tue Mar 15	
Wed Mar 16	
Thu Mar 17	
Fri Mar 18	Full Moon in Elder
Sat Mar 19	
Sun Mar 20	SPRING EQUINOX
Mon Mar 21	

Tue Mar 22

Wed Mar 23

Thu Mar 24

Fri Mar 25

Sat Mar 26

Sun Mar 27

Mon Mar 28

Tue Mar 29   Ash to Hawthorn day

ASH
The Triumph of Dawn

Guardian of the East

DAYS OF
HAWTHORN
9 degrees Aries
to 27 degrees Aries

Wed Mar 30	First full day of Hawthorn
Thu Mar 31	
Fri Apr 1	New Moon
Sat Apr 2	
Sun Apr 3	
Mon Apr 4	
Tue Apr 5	
Wed Apr 6	
Thu Apr 7	
Fri Apr 8	

Sat Apr 9

Sun Apr 10

Mon Apr 11

Tue Apr 12

Wed Apr 13

Thu Apr 14

Fri Apr 15

Sat Apr 16   Full Moon in Pine

Sun Apr 17   Hawthorn to Oak day

HAWTHORN
Proving One's Worth

Pioneer of the Blossoming Days

DAYS OF OAK

27 degrees Aries
to 15 degrees Taurus

BELTANE

Mon Apr 18	First full day of Oak
Tue Apr 19	
Wed Apr 20	
Thu Apr 21	
Fri Apr 22	
Sat Apr 23	
Sun Apr 24	
Mon Apr 25	
Tue Apr 26	
Wed Apr 27	

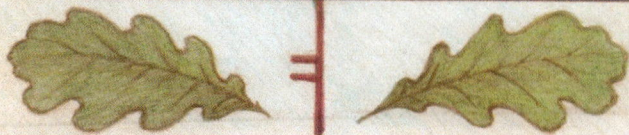

Thu Apr 28

Fri Apr 29

Sat Apr 30   New Moon

Sun May 1

Mon May 2

Tue May 3

Wed May 4

Thu May 5   Oak to Holly day

BELTANE

OAK
Strength and Endurance

The First Herald of Beltane

NOTE

BOOK

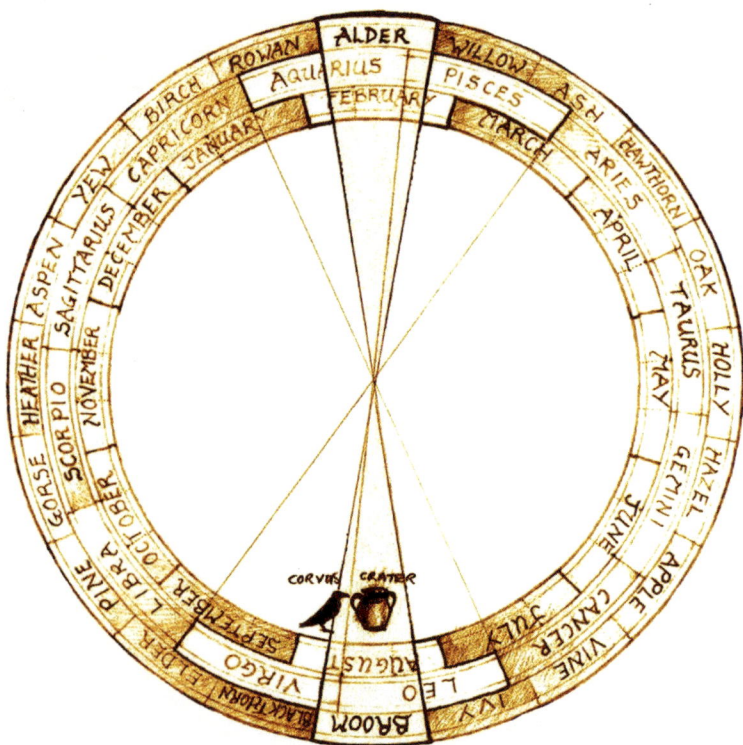

The next issue of *Voices From The Grove (Beltane 2022 to Beltane 2023)* will be dedicated to the god, Bran the Blessed, the Alder tree, and the Cauldron of Annwn.

Contributions can be submitted between Samhain 2021 and Imbolc 2022; just email them to the Editor at

yuri13oct@yahoo.co.uk

For homework and inspiration you can study the Second Branch of *The Mabinogion ~ Branwen the Daughter of Llyr*. There may even be prizes to be won. The name of Branwen's son, Gwern, means Alder; and he is the nephew of Bran. For further information and updates please join the Facebook group,

The Ogham Grove.

Printed in Great Britain
by Amazon